Golf
Hideaways

Golf Hideaways

The Best Courses and Resorts

David Chmiel

RIZZOLI
NEW YORK

First published in the United
States of America in 2004
by Rizzoli International
Publications, Inc.
300 Park Avenue South
New York, NY 10010
www.rizzoliusa.com

Graphic Design: Adam Michaels

Cover photographs:
Front: courtesy of Half Moon
Bay Golf Links
Back: courtesy of Brad Kasselman/
coastphoto.com

2004 2005 2006 2007 /
10 9 8 7 6 5 4 3 2 1

Distributed in the U.S. trade by
St. Martin's Press, New York

Printed in Belgium

ISBN: 0-8478-2612-0

Library of Congress Catalog
Control Number: 2004090082

Introduction 6

Old School

The Equinox, Vermont 10
The Sagamore, New York 14
Seaview Marriott Resort & Spa, New Jersey 18
The Hershey Resort, Pennsylvania 24
Golden Horseshoe Golf Club, Virginia 30
The Homestead, Virginia 36
The Greenbrier, West Virginia 42
Pinehurst Resort, North Carolina 46
Wild Dunes Resort, South Carolina 52
Sea Island Resort, Georgia 58
Grand Cypress Resort, Florida 62
Ponte Vedra Inn & Club, Florida 66
The Broadmoor, Colorado 70
The Boulders, Arizona 76
Four Seasons Resort Scottsdale at Troon North, Arizona 82
La Quinta Resort & Club, California 88
Grand Wailea Resort Hotel & Spa, Hawaii 94
Hyatt Regency Kauai Resort and Spa, Hawaii 98

Opulent

Nemacolin Woodlands Resort & Spa, Pennsylvania 104
Kiawah Island Golf Resort, South Carolina 110
The Ritz-Carlton Lodge, Reynolds Plantation, Georgia 116
The American Club, Wisconsin 122
The Ritz-Carlton, Lake Las Vegas, Nevada 128
Four Seasons Resort Aviara, California 134
The Inn at Spanish Bay, California 140
Pebble Beach Golf Links, California 144
The Ritz-Carlton, Half Moon Bay, California 148
Princeville Resort, Hawaii 154
One&Only Palmilla Resort, Mexico 158
The Ritz-Carlton Golf & Spa Resort, Rose Hall, Jamaica 164
Westin Rio Mar Beach Resort & Golf Club, Puerto Rico 168

Off the Beaten Path

Grand View Lodge, Minnesota 176
Coeur d'Alene Resort, Idaho 182
Bandon Dunes Golf Resort, Oregon 188
Sunriver Resort, Oregon 194
The Fairmont Chateau Whistler, Canada 200

Index 206
Photo Credits 207
Acknowledgments 208

Introduction

Decades ago, an old friend was railing against the headway that tennis appeared to be making on people who'd heretofore had the better sense to play golf. Veins popping, voice booming, he bellowed, "When is the last time you ever heard anyone talk about the great tennis courts of the world?" And while we all agreed quickly and vociferously, partly because we fully concurred but primarily because we really wanted him to get off the table, I was struck by just how lucky I was. Here I was, the grandson of coal miners (one who made it out and one who didn't), in the company of people who'd traveled the world with their golf bags for no reason other than to return home to a computer and recount their adventures for people who might never see these sanctified grounds. It's a world of experiences, where spectacular golf meets fabulous food and wine, where sunsets with bagpipers bleed into discourses on golf-course design and tall tales of holes conquered and promises to get to courses not yet tested.

In the years since, I've traveled many roads, literally and figuratively: I've taken low-budget trips across the country, stopping along the way to check out courses new and old, visiting resorts just opened or in their second century of existence. I've been fortunate enough to be whisked away by private plane (while trying mightily to act unimpressed) and dropped down in a five-star tropical sanctuary. I've also made many research excursions in between those extremes, chasing courses and daylight to shoehorn in as many new experiences as I could manage. Regardless of how many trips I've taken, reaching a new destination and getting to wander in and around unfamiliar territory never loses its allure.

Centuries ago, golf travel from the Caribbean to Canada was reserved as an elitist perk. Today, however, because of a shrinking globe, generations of increasing affluence, and a desire to find new experiences, golf travel has become big business and even bigger fun. The fun has taken on a different feel, too. The days of "Let's play thirty-six holes, eat and drink ourselves silly, and plunk down face-first on the bed" are gone (for the most part, anyway). Today's golf traveler is dedicated to taking full advantage of the resort experience. Since more couples are taking golf vacations together—as golfers, adventurers, and fitness and spa enthusiasts—the resort experience for men has become more inclusive and now offers attractions away from the golf course.

This book is arranged into three sections: Old School, Opulent, and Off the Beaten Path. Whether in tone or longevity, the Old School resorts feature a nod to gentility, paying homage to the days of jackets and ties in the dining room, drinks on the veranda, and an easy peacefulness and leisurely pace. The golf courses are some of the nation's oldest and most respected, and the resorts themselves are full of modern-day amenities in traditional settings. The Opulent resorts feature some of the best in modern golf-course design, but when the round is over, your day is just getting started; you'll be heading into extreme sports, fitness workouts, and the latest in wellness, relaxation, pampering, and primping techniques. The Off the Beaten Path resorts offer a little bit of both worlds but provide their unique experiences in some parts of North America that you might not otherwise consider visiting. Some of these destinations offer the comfort of an old friend, welcoming you back for another visit. While some might surprise you, and others will inspire you to keep looking for new challenges, all end with the shared experience of fine wining and dining (sometimes the most difficult decision is choosing from among these resorts' eateries).

Old School

The hotels and lodges that once served as sanctuary for George Washington, Thomas Jefferson, and other political and commercial leaders of our burgeoning nation boasted leisure activities such as croquet and fox hunting. But an old game made its way from Scotland during this continental infancy and the untamed terrain around these grand dames of United States hostelry was converted into golf courses. The resorts in this category combine traditional course design—by golf course architect greats such as Donald Ross, Walter Travis, Seth Raynor, and Robert Trent Jones Sr.—with genteel off-the-course amenities.

10

14

18

24

30

36

42

46

52

58

62

66

70

76

82

88

94

98

The Equinox
Manchester Village, Vermont

The Equinox
3567 Main Street
Manchester Village, VT 05254
Tel.: (800) 362-4747
Fax: (802) 362-4700
www.equinoxresort.com

Designer: **Walter Travis**

Date opened: **1927, with 1992 redesign by Rees Jones**

Number of holes: **18**

Fees: **$48–$125, depending on season**

Yardage/par: **6,423 yards, par-71**

Rating/slope: **71.3/129**

Pro shop: **Fully appointed stock of apparel and equipment and a good source for warm clothing if you should run into a cold snap**

Golf instruction: **For individual or group sessions, run through the Golf Schools of Scottsdale group**

Driving range/putting green: **Two large putting greens are built in the shadow of the clubhouse, range offers comfortable place to prepare or just practice**

Rentals: **Clubs**

For the better part of the last decade, this southern Vermont staple nestled between the Taconic and Green Mountains has been the poster child for corporate synergy. In 1992 the Guinness Corporation bought the resort, saving it from twenty years of crippling financial struggles. That name resonates with thirsty golfers and traveling golfers alike, since the brewing giant also owns the Gleneagles Resort in the Scottish Highlands. The U.S. sister course was renamed for the Scottish resort and Rees Jones was brought in to give it a $3.5 million thorough but loving renovation.

Another $6.5 million was spent on the hotel and the 1,300-acre resort. The result has reenergized Manchester Village and given people more reason than ever to visit. Of course, it didn't work out so well for the first owner, William Marsh, proprietor of Marsh Tavern. Marsh was a Tory supporter, and when the new colonists realized their own power, they decided that his property would have to be seized as their own. More than two centuries later, however, the Marsh Tavern still stands. Today it provides a place to gather for, of course, Yankee pot roast and shepherd's pie, but all that comfort food does little to inspire talk of politics among the guests.

IN THE SHADOW OF MOUNT EQUINOX, other synergistic opportunities abound, and they're almost as much fun as playing the golf course. You can get behind the wheel of a Hummer or a Land Rover Discovery at the Off Road at the Equinox School, going over and through logging roads, angling through private trails, and rumbling over specially created obstacles. You can also get outfitted at the Orvis fly-fishing school, where serious anglers can get the kind of video analysis and step-by-step training generally associated with in-depth golf lessons.

For decades the Equinox has been the place where people make their annual golf/foliage pilgrimage; but crisp springs and summers are just as much fun. With downtown Manchester just out the front door, there are plenty of antiquing, dining, and shopping options. When you feel like taking the chill off, you can enroll in a yoga or Pilates class, or get the blood pumping on the cardiovascular and weight-training machines. You can also visit the Avanyu Spa, which offers a variety of traditional treatments as well as some with a bit of local flavor—try the maple scrub, which is a mixture of maple sugar, antioxidants, and vitamins aimed at providing a healthy glow.

IN THE RESORT'S SECOND CENTURY of existence, the owners figured this golf thing might have a future. Walter Travis, the first American to win the British

Amateur, was commissioned in 1926 to design the 18-hole course. His layout was a huge success and became a staple in northeastern golf. Over the years, however, the course got lost under a tangle of overgrown vegetation and neglectful ownership. With the Guinness investment all that changed. The course was repositioned in the Gleneagles name, which meant that there had to be a significant upgrade in quality.

Jones's work on the reclamation project resulted in the stretching of the par-71 course to 6,423 yards. He found bunkers that had been lost or ignored and added some more of his own, doubling the total to 112. He also upgraded the drainage of the course, which can be spongy early in the season. From the first tee, the front nine leads you on a fairly straightforward path to the Taconic Mountains. Things get decidedly more difficult on the way back to the hotel, especially on the par-3 fourteenth. From the elevated tee, it plays only 123 yards, but it feels as though the ball takes forever, as it appears to parachute slowly to the green. The seventeenth and eighteenth holes are tricky dogleg lefts that will lead to big scores if you try to bite off too much from the corner. Make a birdie here and you've earned your Guinness.

Whether it's some relaxing time spent lakeside at the foot of the Green Mountains or a fireside game of chess in the lobby, the Equinox's Revolutionary War–era roots imbue your stay with a sense of history.

The Sagamore
Bolton Landing, New York

The Sagamore
110 Sagamore Road
Bolton Landing, NY 12814
Tel.: (800) 358-3585
Fax: (518) 743-6036
www.thesagamore.com

Designer: **Donald Ross**

Date opened: **1928**

Number of holes: **18**

Fees: **$105 (weekday), $115 (weekend)**

Yardage/par: **6,794 yards, par-70**

Rating/slope: **73.8/137**

Pro shop: **Full selection of apparel and equipment**

Golf instruction: **For individual or group sessions**

Driving range/putting green: **Scenic range with natural-grass tees, putting greens that approximate the smallish undulating greens on the course**

Rentals: **Clubs and shoes**

Dating back to 1883, The Sagamore, built on the shores of Lake George in the middle of the Adirondack Mountains, served as a getaway for the wealthy from various northeastern cities. Nothing, not even two fires that turned the hotel into rubble, could stop the moneyed from figuring out ways to keep the place running. Now, after all that trouble, the hotel has at least earned its rightful place as a National Historic Landmark. After a $75-million renovation a little more than a century after it welcomed its first guests, the resort continues to distinguish itself as an old-school favorite.

To call it an old-school favorite, however, is a disservice since it has struck a great balance between rustic charm and twenty-first-century amenities. After choosing to hang out at a wooded lake, you should expect plenty of swimming, fishing, and hiking. Speaking of hiking, the Donald Ross course, circa 1928, is a beautiful walk in the woods, a walk that could also entail trekking from one side to the other on the slick hogback or inverted saucer greens after a slippery chip or forceful putt. The course is fair, the kind of historic gem you can enjoy repeatedly during your stay.

One continuing tradition at The Sagamore is the Morgan, a seventy-two-foot wooden party boat that goes out for public or private meal or booze cruises. The yacht provides a great post-round sunset option for relaxing and enjoying the crisp air.

THE SAGAMORE, one hour from Albany and four hours from New York City, is a rustic treasure. The one-hundred-room Victorian hotel, built for the third time in 1930 (after fires in 1893 and 1914 destroyed the wooden structure), showcases natural furnishings. The resort spreads into the woods with 240 rooms in lodges offering camp-style furnishings and fireplaces. One special option for a family or group of friends is the historic Wapanak Castle, a six-bedroom, four-bathroom home next to the lake near the hotel; it sleeps twelve and features two terraces offering views of Lake George.

Once you pick your lodging, you can choose from a ton of activities. Great Escape Amusement Park offers a boardwalk, shopping, and the Steamin' Demon, a scream-inducing roller coaster. The glass-enclosed fitness center provides cardiovascular and weight-training machines. Classes are offered here in everything from tai chi and yoga to nutritional training and aqua aerobics (in the heated indoor pool). In addition, spa treatments run from the standard massage and facial options to Jin Shu Jmutsu, in which fingertip pressure is applied to "energy pathways," releasing blocked energy, inspiring emotional balance, and relieving pain. There are acupuncture and palmistry sessions as well, and even a session on intuitive counseling.

Hiking the Adirondack peaks, swimming, fishing, boating, and even snorkeling are available for those who like to spend their vacations out and about.

AFTER A $1-MILLION RENOVATION in 1985, the Donald Ross layout at The Sagamore was restored to its original design. Painstaking care was taken to get the traditional cross-bunkers and deep greenside bunkers refurbished so as to present the proper dose of punishment for misplayed shots.

Your pulse quickens as you stand on the elevated first tee; you are inspired by the view over the lake and out to the Adirondack peaks, but terrified of trying to hit the fairway down below. Sadly, that view is the last you'll have of the lake from the course. The first six holes meander through a meadow of Scottish heather, but by the seventh hole the free ride is over, as the hardwood trees tighten the fairways. There is plenty of water on the back side, making position, not length, the key to scoring well. The seventeenth hole will be sporting a new tee in 2004, stretching the par-5 past five hundred yards. Ross placed two large bunkers on the dogleg-right eighteenth, precisely where they can do the most damage—in the left corner of the fairway to catch the cautious player and in the right front edge of the green where most approach shots fade ingloriously. As you finish your first post-round drink, however, you will be glad to have another chance tomorrow to beat this straight-forward piece of Ross history.

Left: Donald Ross designed The Sagamore's course, which winds through woods and provides views of Lake George. Above: The front lawn extends down to the lake, while the Adirondack Mountains loom in the background.

Seaview Marriott Resort & Spa
Galloway Township, New Jersey

Seaview Marriott Resort & Spa
401 South New York Road
Galloway Township, NJ 08205
Tel.: (609) 652-1800
Fax: (609) 652-2307
www.seaviewgolf.com

Designer: **Hugh Wilson, with bunkers by Donald Ross and redesign by Bob Cupp Jr. (Bay Course); William Flynn, with renovation by William Gordon (Pines Course)**

Date opened: **1914**

Number of holes: **36**

Fees: **$100–$175**

Yardage/par: **6,8247 yards, par-71 (Bay); 6,731 yards, par-72 (Pines)**

Rating/slope: **70.7/122 (Bay); 72.4/131 (Pines)**

Pro shop: **Small, well-kept shop provides good collection of apparel and hard-goods; the resort even has its own plaid, available for sweaters**

Golf instruction: **For individual or group sessions, at the new Faldo Learning Center**

Driving range/putting green: **Generous 22-acre range is matched with extensive short-game/bunker area; four putting greens between the courses**

Rentals: **Clubs**

It's like standing in the gas-lit early twentieth century while taking in the neon twenty-first: From Seaview Marriott, built in 1910, you can look across Reeds Bay and see Atlantic City (of course, astronauts orbiting the earth can see Atlantic City, too). Whichever side of the juxtaposition you prefer is your decision, but a stay at Seaview won't have you losing your first fifty-dollar bill forty minutes after the valet brings the car around.

The 297-room colonial-style resort, site of the 1942 PGA Championship, conjures a long-gone era. Jackets and ties are still a necessity in the main dining room. The rooms are full of antiques and the kind of four-poster beds that require a small stepping stool to get under the covers. While the courses boast an impeccable historical pedigree, today's players don't boast about overpowering these short but tricky layouts. The salt breezes lend a milder winter air to Seaview, giving you the chance to flee the snow and chill without having to jump on a plane.

Need another juxtaposition? Like many resorts that enjoy recounting visits by various dignitaries, it is made known that Seaview has been frequented by President Warren G. Harding, Princess Grace, and Bob Dylan.

SEAVIEW MARRIOTT RESORT & SPA is an hour's drive from Philadelphia and about two hours from New York City. It is recognized by the National Trust Historic Hotels of America for the preservation of its historical integrity and ambience. The main dining room, a circular space with huge glass windows, provides a great look at the glitz across Reeds Bay. The informal Grill Room has the feel of a pub and serves comfort food. The Lobby Lounge has a piano around which people have been known to gather and share a song or two. Don't miss the delicious summer seafood catches in the Oval Room off the bar.

Despite the commitment to Seaview Marriott's heritage, the resort still added enough of the modern amenities that visitors expect. These include thirty-two bedroom fairway villas, indoor and outdoor pools, and a large fitness room complete with a variety of cardiovascular and weight-training machines, as well as free weights. In addition, visitors need only enter through the Red Door—the Elizabeth Arden Red Door Spa, that is—for a variety of soothing treatments. Aside from the traditional pedicure, manicure, and hair treatments, you can also get massages and an assortment of exfoliating and revitalizing therapies.

Left: The fairways are guarded by pines on the course that bears their name, but the green complexes allow shots to roll up onto the greens.
Above: After making a grand entrance into the colonial-style resort, you can get a glimpse of the Atlantic City glitz across the bay.

SEAVIEW'S BAY COURSE, home to the LPGA's ShopRite Classic for the last fourteen years, has long been credited to Ross. Recently, however, it was discovered that Hugh Wilson, who designed the fabled Merion Golf Club in suburban Philadelphia, had tackled its routing. A redesign by Robert Cupp Jr. was completed in 1998, including a restoration to the original Ross bunker designs that had been lost in translation over the years. Playing just 6,247 yards from the tips, the course isn't one that will reward players who just try to blast away off the tee. The virtually treeless course features open runways into tear-shaped greens on holes into the wind to aid players running the ball onto the green. On downwind holes, such as the 300-yard fifth and 280-yard eighth, pot bunkers front the greens to make players float shots to the tightly tucked pins.

The Pines Course began as a third nine, built in 1931 by William Flynn, the former Merion superintendent who eventually began to design courses. Flynn's nine was matched with the Bay Course's front nine to serve as the routing for the PGA Championship, which was Sam Snead's first major victory. The 6,731-yard course is physically tighter than the Bay Course, but the psychological squeeze might be even more significant since the scrub pines and abundant sand (added by William Gordon in his 1957 redesign) makes it feel like you're threading the needle off the tee. If you can keep it in the fairway, the back nine at the Pines gives you a great shot at scoring well. The 515-yard tenth and 500-yard eighteenth offer you a chance to open and close with birdies, ones that you might need after tackling the back-to-back par-3 fifteenth and sixteenth holes, each of which top out at more than two hundred yards.

The Bay Course, home to the LPGA's ShopRite Classic for the last fourteen years, features small greens guarded by a variety of bunkers originally designed by legendary golf course architect Donald Ross.

The Hershey Resort
Hershey, Pennsylvania

The Hershey Resort
100 Hotel Road
Hershey, PA 17033
Tel.: (800) HERSHEY
Fax: (717) 534-8887
www.hersheypa.com

Designer: **Maurice McCarthy (West Course); George Fazio (East Course)**

Date opened: **1930 (West); 1984 (East)**

Number of holes: **36, but eighteen-hole public course also available and nine-hole executive course available on grounds of Hershey Lodge**

Fees: **$75–$95 (West); $60–$80 (East)**

Yardage/par: **6,860 yards, par-73 (West); 7,061 yards, par-71 (East)**

Ratings/slope: **73.1/131 (West); 73.6/128 (East)**

Pro shop: **The pro shop offers everything from shoes to putters, as well as a variety of apparel featuring the Hershey logo**

Golf instruction: **For individual or group sessions**

Driving range/putting green: **Good range, large putting green**

Rentals: **Clubs**

Milton Hershey returned from a trip to Europe with one goal: He wanted to add a grand-scale hotel on top of the Blue Mountain foothills from which visitors could see the town that he was building one chocolate bar at a time. More than seventy years later, the Hershey Hotel is as much a central Pennsylvania staple as the little kisses wrapped in aluminum foil. Hershey was a genius, making a mass-produced confection that nobody could live without, and he continued to find new ways to identify what people were looking for before they even realized they wanted it.

Since that time, the perch Hershey built has been thriving, having been reinvented like the kiss with the almond inside. There must be something inspiring in the chocolate that the visitors and locals inhale here. This old-school institution, the place where Ben Hogan—yes, *that* Ben Hogan—was once the head golf professional, and the place that hosted the 1940 PGA Championship, has made some modifications to the courses to keep golf fanatics happy. The hotel that keeps an eye on the sweetest company in the country has made the switch from dowdy grand dame to good-life destination.

Today, as you linger over breakfast, you toy with the idea of reading the paper while breathing in the chocolate-scented air, giving in to the pull of the roller coasters twirling at the bottom of the hill, or opting for an indulgent Chocolate Fondue Wrap (a spa treatment, not a snack). Instead, you feel the need to get a tee time at the course that has been a regular stop on the Nationwide Tour.

THREE HOURS FROM NEW YORK CITY and two hours from Philadelphia and Washington, the Hershey Resort is quickly becoming a place to escape hectic schedules and harried living, where you can say with a straight face, "I am going to get some chocolate treatments," and it has nothing to do with inhaling a box of brownies. The aforementioned Chocolate Fondue Wrap, comprised of warm moor mud and essence of cocoa, is meant to revitalize and nourish the skin as well as calm the subject. How about the Chocolate Bean Polish? Sit back and relax while you are exfoliated with cocoa bean husks and walnut shells and rubbed down with a cocoa body moisturizer. Lest you claim candy bias, you can also sign up for a Strawberry Parfait Scrub or Peppermint Salt Scrub.

This four-star, AAA four-diamond destination has also earned its stripes with the Historic Hotels of America. The hallways and rooms are full of these historic reminders, from old pictures and original paintings on the walls to the cherry furniture and traditional decor that fill the rooms. The main dining room features a circular design so that every person is afforded an unobstructed view of the resort's formal gardens. Not surprisingly, the chocolate theme follows you all over the hotel, from the casual Cocoa Beanery restaurant to the Iberian Lounge, famous for its chocolate martini.

Above: The West Course, built in 1930, gives players the chance to land the ball in front of the green and run it up to the hole. Left: The George Fazio–designed East Course.

THE WEST COURSE at the Hershey Resort has been the site for some historic moments in golf, such as when Byron Nelson beat Sam Snead, one-up, to win the 1940 PGA Championship. Home since 1997 to the Nationwide Tour's Hershey Open, this layout has always proved to be a solid test for players of every level. The resort and the course earned *Golf Magazine*'s Silver Medal Resort designation in 1999.

Designed by Maurice McCarthy, the West Course provides a bird's-eye view of the town, including play atop the hill on the front lawn of Milton Hershey's estate, High Point Mansion. This 6,860-yard, par-73 course has tree-lined but generous fairways. But the challenging hazards make the large undulating and fast greens treacherous. As is generally the case with older courses, being in the proper position for your approach shot makes the difference between birdie chances and bogey putts.

The par-71 East Course features three man-made lakes and more than one hundred bunkers, which can create a long day for anyone having directional difficulties. Designed by George Fazio, it provides an even tougher test than its more mature sister course. In addition to the two resort courses, the Parkview Course, located just across the road and adjacent to the amusement park, is a par-71 layout regarded as one of central Pennsylvania's most challenging public courses. Full of tree-lined doglegs and elevated greens, it's an interesting course. And after the second hole, you learn to ignore the screaming teenagers hurtling upside down from the roller coasters at Hershey Park.

Above: The East (shown here) and West courses at Hershey include elevation changes that provide views of the landscape of central Pennsylvania.
Right: The West Course's fourth hole was built to provide a view of Highpoint Mansion, home of the chocolate company's founder, Milton Hershey.

Golden Horseshoe Golf Club
Colonial Williamsburg, Virginia

Golden Horseshoe Golf Club
401 South England Street
Williamsburg, VA 23188
Tel.: (757) 220-7696
Fax: (757) 565-8840
www.colonialwilliamsburg.com

Designer: **Robert Trent Jones Sr. (Gold Course and Spotswood Golf Course); Rees Jones (Green Course)**

Date opened: **1963 (Gold); 1991 (Green); 1964 (Spotswood)**

Number of holes: **18 (Gold and Green); 9 (Spotswood)**

Fees: **Variety of packages available**

Yardage/par: **6,817 yards, par-71 (Gold); 7,120 yards, par-72 (Green); 1,865 yards, par-31 (Spotswood)**

Rating/slope: **73.6/138 (Gold); 73.4/134 (Green); 31/105 (Spotswood)**

Pro shop: **Full-service shop provides a variety of equipment and apparel**

Golf instruction: **For individual or group sessions; *Golf Digest* multi-day programs also available**

Driving range/putting green: **Full-service practice area**

Rentals: **Clubs and shoes**

Just a nine-iron from the colonial village so captivatingly recreated each day, the legend of the Golden Horseshoe is relived, not by the colonists who made an expedition in 1724 through the four mountain chains converging in Virginia (the hardy explorers were reportedly each given a golden horseshoe in honor of their fortitude), but by the intrepid souls emboldened to survive the modern-day Jones golf course.

The recently completed multimillion-dollar renovation of the five lodging options in this Colonial Williamsburg complex offers the choice of old-world spirit or twenty-first-century luxury. Guests can replicate an eighteenth-century stay in the Williamsburg Inn or Colonial Guesthouses or choose to spend time in the Woodlands Hotel & Suites, built in the middle of a forty-acre pine forest. But back to our intrepid golfers who, while trying to navigate the world-famous Gold Course (designed by Robert Trent Jones Sr.) or twelve-year-old Green Course (designed by son Rees Jones), may actually feel just as surrounded by pines. From rustic to regal, the Golden Horseshoe Golf Club ties together the nation's living history and its golf present and future as a four-star destination.

IMAGE SITTING DOWN to dinner at one of George Washington's favorite eateries and talking about your three-putt or career drive. At Christiana Campbell's, the first United States president's regular haunt, specialties such as sherried crab stew, sea pye (a dish of crab, fin-fish, shrimp, lobster, and cream), cabbage slaw, and sweet potato muffins are offered. Because it is a family destination, the restaurants at the Golden Horseshoe provide every permutation of food and formality in its ten other restaurants, from the jacket-and-tie Regency Room to the Huzzah! Pizzah parlor.

The resort offers a variety of activities once you get off the golf course or finish the rounds of the historical and educational tours. Indoor and outdoor pools are located throughout the complex. The Tazewell Club Fitness Center is a hub for those seeking a full weight-training/aerobic workout (including post-session sauna, steam, and whirlpool staples). Treatment fanatics can get a variety of massages or spa services, including body wraps. Nature lovers can meander through a number of trails designed for runners, walkers, or bikers.

The Golden Horseshoe offers 1,073 rooms and suites in its five hotels. The world-famous four-star Williamsburg Inn has been newly refurbished, retaining some of the original eighteenth-century furnishings. The sixty-two rooms average five hundred square feet, and the Restoration Bar and Terrace Room offer cocktails and a tearoom, respectively. The Governor's Inn is a family-friendly lodging option, while the Colonial Houses, Williamsburg Lodge, and Woodlands Hotel & Suites provide a variety of options for those looking for more amenities.

Clockwise, from far left: Rees Jones designed the tight tree-lined Green Course in 1991; his father, Robert Trent Jones Sr., created the Gold Course; the charm of Jones's Gold Course matches that of the Golden Horseshoe's properties.

ACCORDING TO THE LEGEND from which this resort takes its name, the colonial explorers who survived their Virginia journey received golden horseshoes inscribed with the words *"Sic juvat transcendere montes,"* or "How delightful it is to cross mountains." Any golfer making it through the challenging but walkable (for those not afraid to experience what has become a lost art in resort golf) Gold and Green courses could claim they deserve a horseshoe of their own.

The Gold Course is carved through the woods, leaving tight shots from the tees onto sloped fairway landing areas; then it gets difficult. The small rolling greens allow the grounds crew to be creative (read: sadistic) with pin placements. The 169-yard par-3 sixteenth hole gives players a bird's-eye view (literally, since the drop from tee to green is best navigated with a set of wings) of the first island green built by Robert Trent Jones Sr. Its pond is bordered by the twelfth green and continues along to the left of the seventeenth hole.

Rees Jones finished the Green Course in 1991, and although it is longer than his father's design, he was kind enough to cut down a few more pines on each side of the holes, providing wider fairways, framed more forgivingly by "shoulders" or subtle mounds that help keep slightly off-line shots from kicking deep into the trees. Don't be fooled entirely, though, because those shoulders can also dump balls into the many bunkers that dot the course. He also shaved much of the open grassy throats into the greens, which allows players to either hit high soft shots into the pin or play lower running shots that can run to the hole. The sixth hole, however, borrows some of the all-carry tendencies of which his father was fond. The 450-yard par-4 requires an approach shot over a ravine into a green framed by a horseshoe of trees. If the final hole, a 531-yard par-5, looks longer than it is, it's because it narrows all the way to the green, creating a vanishing point effect that makes the third shot into the pot bunker–pocked green feel as though it has to be squeezed through a two-foot opening.

Clockwise, from top left: Robert Trent Jones Sr.'s island green at the Gold Course's par-3 sixteenth hole; the resort's colonial interior; the dining room; the comfort of your suite awaits you after a hard day's play.

The Homestead
Hot Springs, Virginia

The Homestead
U.S. Route 220, Main Street
P.O. Box 2000
Hot Springs, VA 24445
Tel.: (800) 838-1766
or (540) 839-1766
Fax: (540) 839-1670
www.thehomestead.com

Designer: **Donald Ross (Old Course); Williams S. Flynn (Cascades Course); Robert Trent Jones Sr. (Lower Cascades Course)**

Date opened: **1892 (Old); 1923 (Cascades); 1963 (Lower Cascades)**

Number of holes: **54**

Fees: **$95**

Yardage/par: **6,211 yards, par-72 (Old); 6,679 yards, par-70 (Cascades); 6,752 yards, par-72 (Lower Cascades)**

Rating/slope: **69.7/120 (Old); 73.1/137 (Cascades); 72.6/134 (Lower Cascades)**

Pro shop: **Features an extensive array of merchandise, from golf balls and equipment to high-end apparel**

Golf instruction: **For individual or group sessions, at the renowned Golf Advantage School**

Driving range/putting green: **Good range, large putting green**

Rentals: **Clubs**

The Homestead was born ten years before the American Revolution on Allegheny Mountain terrain that rises and falls in leafy glory regardless of the season, and boasts therapeutic hot springs that feel as though they can cure what ails you. Even a twenty-three-year-old George Washington, then leader of the Virginia militia, visited the site in 1755, when just a few cabins dotted the territory.

In the 249 years since, The Homestead has become America's grand dame of golf resorts, a place to enjoy everything from lawn bowling and archery to golf and off-season skiing. The 506-room hotel offers the grandeur of "high tee," so to speak, followed by casual dining at the restaurant that bears the name of former caddie and one of Virginia's greatest resources, the late Sam Snead. The hot springs allow you to soak in one-hundred-degree waters, soothing tired muscles and giving you a chance to relive the experience that many United States presidents since the nation's first have had.

The aptly named Old Course predates the United States Golf Association. The Donald Ross design boasts the nation's oldest first tee in continuous use. The Cascades and Lower Cascades courses present tight and wide fairways, respectively, cutting a spectacular swath through the woods and fields in the Allegheny chain.

THE ENORMOUS GEORGIAN-INSPIRED HOTEL at The Homestead rises at the foothills as the centerpiece from which all activities begin. The resort has recently completed renovations of all of its 506 guest rooms and suites. Traditional furnishings, thick patterned carpets, and floral draperies mirror the Georgian architecture. Each wing of this national historic landmark has been carefully decorated with different themes, and the rooms all feature antique pieces and original artwork.

The lobby of the hotel even has a livery stand, where you can arrange horseback rides and tours of the property in a horse-drawn surrey. The indoor pools, fed by the hot springs, give men and women the chance to imagine themselves in eighteenth-century Virginia. Some would say the men's pool, built in 1761, might be showing its age, but it really should be thought of as revealing its history. A variety of thoroughly modern treatments are available from head to toe in the spa.

The main dining room is still a jacket-and-tie staple, featuring great service, an extensive wine list, and elegant fare. If you have a hankering for a steak or a chop, you can't go wrong at Sam Snead's Tavern, across the street from the resort, where the atmosphere, memorabilia, and food mix perfectly.

The outdoor activities on this 15,000-acre compound include hayrides, guided caving expeditions, canoeing down the Jackson River, and hiking along the Cascades Gorge, which has thirteen waterfalls. If that's not enough, you can visit the falconry school or Challenge Course, an outward bound–style adventure for families and friends.

Clockwise, from far left: Thomas Jefferson was among the early visitors to the hot springs at The Homestead, and hundreds of years later guests are still enjoying the healing waters, which fill the resort's pools; the well-manicured gardens of the resort; the Georgian-inspired main building rises from behind the trees; the tiny greens of the Old and Cascades courses are reminders of some of the earliest courses built in the United States.

THE CASCADES COURSE at The Homestead, designed in 1923 by William S. Flynn, has remained a top-fifty course since the lists were created. The spectacular scenery is evident from a number of different vantage points since the first thirteen holes feature drops of as much as one hundred feet from tee to green. The 434-yard dogleg-right twelfth hole drops precipitously from the tee to a fairway that runs along the Swift River. The course boasts an odd configuration, with five par-5s and five par-3s.

That is not the only quirky course design at The Homestead; Ross's Old Course features six par-3s, six par-4s, and six par-5s. The Old Course's configuration could be the result of its evolution, since it started as a six-hole layout, and continued to grow as more guests caught the golf bug. The course was revamped admirably by Rees Jones, whose father designed the newest course, the Lower Cascades Course, in 1963. It features wide fairways, well-bunkered greens, and breathtaking scenery.

When you're warming up on the nice flat practice range, enjoy it because that will be the last even stance you have on any of the courses (sometimes even when you're putting). The uphill, downhill, and side hill lies are constants. There is one other constant; no matter where you go on The Homestead golf courses (and pubs), you can feel Sam Snead's presence. It is estimated that Snead played more than three thousand rounds at the course, and many of those rounds came after he hustled a game with visitors over breakfast or lunch. He always played hard, always found a way to win, and always collected his bets. There is no record of George Washington hustling any golfers during any post-Revolution rounds.

Above: The Lower Cascades Course runs in and out of the trees and in front of the Allegheny Mountains, which provide a dramatic backdrop for any season. Right: The Homestead's scenic surroundings also provide ample outdoor activities for active vacationers after they get off the golf course.

The Greenbrier
White Sulphur Springs, West Virginia

The Greenbrier
300 West Main Street
White Sulphur Springs, WV 24986
Tel.: (800) 453-4858
Fax: (304) 536-7854
www.greenbrier.com

Designer: **Seth Raynor and George O'Neil (Greenbrier Course);**
C. B. MacDonald (Old White Course); Alex Findlay (Meadows Course)

Date opened: **1924, with 1977 renovation by Jack Nicklaus (Greenbrier);**
1913 (Old White); 1910, with 1962 expansion by Dick Wilson and 1999
update by Bob Cupp (Meadows)

Number of holes: **54 holes**

Fees: **$135**

Yardage/par: **6,675 yards, par-72 (Greenbrier); 6,652 yards, par-70**
(Old White); 6,807 yards, par-71 (Meadows)

Rating/slope: **73.1/135 (Greenbrier); 72/128 (Old White); 72.4/128**
(Meadows)

Pro shop: **Fully stocked shops**

Golf instruction: **For individual or group sessions, with PGA and LPGA**
professionals

Driving range/putting green: **The 65,000-square-foot range even**
includes a practice fairway bunker; two practice greens provide
plenty of ground to work on long putts

Rentals: **Clubs and shoes**

Many resorts can boast about having eight hundred rooms with antique appointments and the healing waters of sulphur springs, and plenty can go on about having three historic courses (the first of which was built in 1913). The field starts shrinking, however, when they tout hosting a Ryder Cup or giving visitors access to falconry, off-road driving, and whitewater-rafting lessons. Toss in bowling alleys and a 1780 opening date, and it doesn't take long to call roll. But The Greenbrier always wins as a unique resort when it pulls out the trump card—a (formerly) top-secret underground "government relocation facility," commonly known as a bunker to all you baby boomers.

The existence of the 112,000-square-foot "Project Greek Island" bunker, built during the height of Cold War America's tensions, was disclosed in 1992, and daily tours are available for guests. But once you get the fascinating tour out of your system, there is really no reason to spend a non-dining moment of your stay indoors. The golf courses, the original designs of which have been spruced up by Dick Wilson and Jack Nicklaus, are spectacular. Different layouts present varied views and new challenges as a result of their different topography. The list of other available activities makes some people yearn for a hammock, but there is plenty of time to rest—away from this remarkable historic West Virginia property.

THE SULPHUR SPRINGS, touted since the eighteenth century as a miracle cure-all for just about anything that ails you, are available in a variety of soaks aimed at soothing sore muscles and relieving tension. Not to ruin the truly therapeutic karma that the sulphur springs bring, but if you remember your high-school chemistry, sulphur equals essence of rotten eggs. But hey, no nasal pain, no revitalization gained. In addition to the sulphur treatments, the spa provides everything from workout sessions with personal trainers to "body booster" treatments, which include the Athlete's Cocoon and the Travel Fatigue, each providing warm soothing wraps, rubs with oils, and reflexology massages aimed at helping you rid your body of the negative, muscle-tightening stresses of everyday life and athletic pursuits in favor of total relaxation.

Once you've been kneaded, oiled, and refreshed, you can stroll around the 6,500-acre grounds and decide what you'll be trying tomorrow. You could also simply stroll through the massive Georgian-style resort, soaking up the gentility and romantic touches decorating the walls and floors. From furnishings to artwork, The Greenbrier wraps you in attitude adjustment. The main dining room provides elegant atmosphere and the best in continental dining, while the Tavern Room and next-door Wine Bar and Wine Cellar offer welcome after-dinner spots. And while The Greenbrier makes you feel as though you're in a movie from another time, you can actually live vicariously through silver-screen heroes by enjoying the resort's nightly showing of first-run titles.

THE GREENBRIER COURSE is the only course in the world to have hosted both the Ryder Cup (1979) and Solheim Cup (1994) matches. The course is framed by leafy, mature trees—the trees that you "ooh" and "aah" over atop the Allegheny Mountains when you arrive but begin to hate as they appear to squeeze every fairway on the course. Nicklaus's work on the course did nothing to alter the straightforward layout, but there are many all-carry approaches to the slick terraced greens. True to the Nicklaus philoso-

phy in play and design, position is everything and will dictate your score, for better or worse.

The Old White Course is the oldest full layout at the resort. The course's elevated first tee abuts the clubhouse porch, providing a jump start to the nerves for anyone afraid of unveiling his or her full display. MacDonald's layout mirrors his Scottish heritage; the course is laid out in front of you, and the creative player can attack pins with high, soft shots, but it was created to reward players who embrace the Scottish game with low, running shots that land short of the green and roll to the flag.

The Meadows Course, originally built in 1910 as a nine-hole layout, was once known as the Lakeside Course. Wilson converted it to a full-fledged championship layout and it was also the site of a 1999 refurbishing by Bob Cupp that revitalized every bunker on the course; two hundred new trees were added, while twelve trees that had grown too large were removed. The course now stretches to more than 6,800 yards and has become a better complement to the two other courses.

Top, left and right: The Greenbrier, which has hosted the Ryder and Solheim cup international competitions, rises into the clouds that float above the trees of the Allegheny Mountains. Bottom, left and right: The grandeur of the Greenbrier is obvious inside and out.

Pinehurst Resort
Village of Pinehurst, North Carolina

Pinehurst Resort
80 Carolina Vista
Village of Pinehurst, NC 28374
Tel.: (800) ITSGOLF
Fax: (910) 235-8466
www.pinehurst.com

Designer: **Donald Ross (Nos. 1–4); Ellis Maples (No. 5); George and Tom Fazio (No. 6); Rees Jones (No. 7); Tom Fazio (No. 8)**

Date opened: **1898 (No. 1); 1907 (No. 2); 1910 (No. 3); 1919, with 2000 redesign (No. 4); 1961 (No. 5); 1979 (No. 6); 1986, with 2003 renovation (No. 7); 1996 (No. 8)**

Number of holes: **144**

Fees: **$150–$275**

Yardage/par: **6,128 yards, par-70 (No. 1); 6,741 yards, par-71 (No. 2); 5,682 yards, par-70 (No. 3); 6,658 yards, par-72 (No. 4); 6,640 yards, par-72 (No. 5); 6,603 yards, par-72 (No. 6); 7,207 yards, par-72 (No. 7); 6,698 yards, par-72 (No. 8)**

Rating/slope: **69.4/116 (No. 1); 72.8/131 (No. 2); 67.2/115 (No. 3); 72.1/130 (No. 4); 72.2/131 (No. 5); 71.9/130 (No. 6); 72.7/135 (No. 7); 72.4/129 (No. 8)**

Pro shop: **It's hard to leave the shop of this resort, which features everything from clubs and clothes to teddy bears, tumblers, and prints, without buying something bearing Pinehurst's famed "Putter Boy" logo**

Golf instruction: **For individual or group sessions, at The Pinehurst Company Golf Institute; golfers can create their own agenda for improving individual aspects of their games**

Driving range/putting green: **Wide practice range with target greens, bunker, and chipping practice areas, and one of the largest practice greens in the world**

It is hard to believe that James Walker Tufts, the Boston inventor of the soda fountain, philanthropist, and founder of the university that bears his name, bought five thousand acres of overforested, desolate, sandy North Carolina soil in 1895—for five thousand dollars—and actually believed that chilled Yankees would join him there. Of course, he did have a little help; he hired Frederick Law Olmsted (the architect of Central Park) and a young golf course architect named Donald Ross. Olmsted had a reputation, but Ross had inspiration. He was the protégé of Old Tom Morris, the legendary St. Andrews pro. More than a century later, the quaint village Olmsted built remains largely unchanged while Ross's four courses represent half of what is arguably the nation's greatest golf destination. From the 1901 opening of the Carolina, the grand Victorian hotel, through today, the Pinehurst Resort, which encompasses two thousand of those original acres, exudes a gentility, elegance, and simple air.

There are now 510 rooms available at various Pinehurst properties (whether rooms or suites in the Carolina, the Holly, the Manor, or the various villas and condos), and the resort has grown to include luxurious spas and other modern-day amenities. But somehow, it hasn't lost its early twentieth-century vibe. Variety is the key: Whether it's a trip to the Ryder Cup Lounge, the world's best breakfast in the Carolina's dining room, or even the walk down to the storied Pine Crest Inn (once owned by Ross), the town, its residents, and visitors all share a love for golf and the eight courses that brings out the differences and similarities in the sports challenge. From short, tight, and tricky to sprawling, straightforward, and just plain difficult, Pinehurst is full of nuance, detail, and reverence.

FIRST AND FOREMOST, Pinehurst is a place for walkers. Take a caddie on No. 2, the course that will make the top five on just about any seasoned golfer's list, or just explore your surroundings and take in the air because both the resort and the town are best enjoyed on foot. But before you set out on the path to town, head into the Spa at Pinehurst, where you can indulge in anything from thirty-minute soaking baths to the Pine Salt Scrub and Carolina Peach Nourisher treatments. If you have no intention of moving for a while, you could get a Sculpting Seagrove Clay Wrap, in which a warm red clay mask is applied to your entire body. A massage of the body, scalp, and feet follow.

Health-conscious golfers can also receive golf-fitness evaluations, as well as training in golf-specific stretching that can create a more supple swing. For the more advanced enthusiast, classes in yoga and Pilates are also available.

The aforementioned Carolina breakfast is the kind of buffet feast that allows you to spend a long time with the morning paper or simply consume enough food to fuel you through a thirty-six-hole day. The eight other eateries range from the Ryder Cup Lounge, where you can get a drink or casual fare, to the jacket-and-tie elegance of the Holly Inn's 1895 Room, to the pub fare of the Tavern, an authentic Scottish bar.

Above: The Carolina Inn is the stately centerpiece of the Pinehurst Resort.
Left: The eight golf courses feature the designs of generations of the world's best course architects, from Donald Ross to Rees Jones.

MR. TUFTS WAS SMART ENOUGH to hire Mr. Ross, and the rest is golf history. Ross was not given to hyperbole, but he said of Pinehurst's No. 2, "This is the fairest test of championship golf." Of course, he spent decades tweaking the layout, which features pine-lined fairways and convex greens that force golfers to make a variety of shots and then get just as creative in their recovery efforts. The course is a straightforward masterpiece that challenges the player to see Ross's intentions and try to play the angles in order to manage their way around the course. The scene for the memorable showdown between the late Payne Stewart and Phil Mickelson for the 1999 U.S. Open title showed just what the course could take from the world's best, a testament to Ross and Rees Jones, who had done some updating to the course in 1996 to get it Open-ready.

In 1986 Jones designed No. 7. The course, about a mile from the Carolina, features undulating terrain (nearly half the approach shots play uphill) that is bordered by thick native vegetation. The greens are slick and tricky to read. In 2003 Jones finished a year-long renovation of the course. As part of the reworking, he also came across some old blueprints that Ross had used for a course that once existed on the site. As a result, there is now a pot bunker next to the fourth tee in honor of Ross's design.

Tom Fazio built No. 8, known as the Centennial Course, which was unveiled for the resort's hundredth anniversary. The course leaps over and twists through 125 acres of wetlands and freshwater marshes. The greens bear the Ross convex sensibility, but are much larger than those on No. 2.

Above: Pinehurst offers plenty of places to get a cocktail, discuss the day's round, or wander among the artifacts from the resort's storied history as host to championship golf. Right: The scrub pines and needles atop the sandy soil line the holes of the resort's eight courses.

Wild Dunes Resort
Isle of Palms, South Carolina

Wild Dunes Resort
5757 Palm Boulevard
Isle of Palms, SC 29451
Tel.: (888) 845-8926
Fax: (843) 886-2916
www.wilddunes.com

Designer: **Tom Fazio**

Date opened: **1980 (Links Course); 1985 (Harbor Course)**

Number of holes: **36**

Fees: **$70–$185 (Links); $55–$119 (Harbor)**

Yardage/par: **6,722 yards, par-72 (Links); 6,446 yards, par-70 (Harbor)**

Rating/slope: **72.7/131 (Links); 70.9/124 (Harbor)**

Pro shop: **Meets a variety of needs, from casual wear to clubs**

Golf instruction: **For individual or group sessions**

Driving range/putting green: **Good range and putting green**

Rentals: **Clubs available**

The fight for this lush barrier island between the Atlantic Ocean and the Intracoastal Waterway was first fought for during the Revolutionary War, when colonists and members of the Catawba Indian tribe banded together to beat back an attempt by Lord Cornwallis's brigade to reclaim the land in the name of the British crown.

While golfers everywhere have been thanking those who fought so valiantly nearly 230 years ago, sometimes these duffers walk off the two Tom Fazio courses at Wild Dunes Resort feeling as if they'd been in a battle of their own. The resort, which boasts 1,600 acres of private ocean-front property, has become a highly decorated destination. And although there are plenty of high-end options available at Wild Dunes for visitors who are used to being pampered, there are also plenty of options for those who like their vacations a bit more open-ended and are more inclined to hang out on the beach or in a boat. There are more than three hundred villas, or full-fledged homes, while the Boardwalk Inn provides all the amenities you'd expect from a hotel stay.

JUST TWENTY MINUTES from Charleston, Wild Dunes places you within an easy drive of the charming city's fine dining and entertainment options. The low-key resort, however, has plenty of attractions competing for your time. Whether it's a post-round massage at the Island Day Spa, a workout in the fitness room, a visit to the marina for deep-sea fishing, a family sailing or kayaking excursion to some of the nearby islands, or just relaxing on the two miles of private oceanfront property, guests can be as active or as mellow as they please. Lodging offerings include the Boardwalk Inn, a Victorian-style four-star/four-diamond winner made up of ninety-three luxury rooms and suites. The inn's Sea Island Grill provides the best local seafood as well as steaks and chops,

while Edgar's in the Links Clubhouse overlooks four fairways of the Links Course and is a casual place to enjoy low-country cuisine. Edgar's also provides live music five nights a week. For visitors who wish to kick back and relax, the villas and homes provide options of one to six bedrooms, full kitchens, and other homestyle touches.

Left and above: The Links Course, designed by Tom Fazio, provides a challenging route through tall grasses and rolling dunes. It also offers beautiful views of the ocean—and the gusting winds that make its closing holes among the toughest in the southeast.

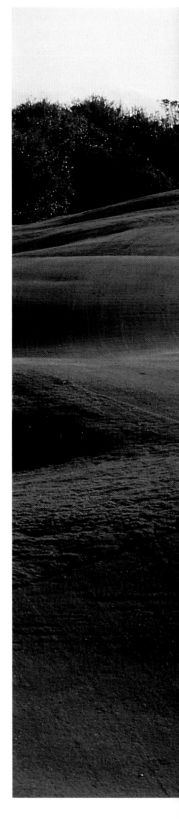

THE LINKS COURSE at Wild Dunes Resort does provide walking golfers with the opportunity to keep the carts stalled near the pro shop. Give the shop forty-eight-hour notice that you'd like to hire a caddie and you'll get even greater satisfaction on this Tom Fazio layout that features massive dunes, windblown native grasses, and sprawling natural hazards. When long hitters get to the tenth tee, feel the wind at their backs, and see the pin a mere 331 yards away, they rarely fight the urge to go for the green and try to start the back nine with a shot at an eagle. They seldom walk away with that eagle, since the wind generally weakens somewhere around the dune that rises to the green. Hacking their ball—if they can even find it—out of the tall grass and sand often leads to double bogey. The smart player will take less club from the tee and be able to spin a wedge close enough to have a good shot at birdie.

Of course, you can't help but try to make plenty of birdies early on the back nine because you know the challenge of the seventeenth and eighteenth holes could easily lead to some very large numbers as you make your way back to the clubhouse. As you advance the ball along the seventeenth, bordered on the left by the Atlantic Ocean, you have to try to keep the ball under the wind or you'll be sorting through the tall grass—once again—on the right. If you make it through the seventeenth without incident, you will then be charged with using the wind to your advantage on the 501-yard dogleg-right closing hole. If you're brave enough to hug the right side of the fairway, you've got a legitimate opportunity to make it to the green in two and two-putt for birdie. When you leave the back of the eighteenth green, you have a great chance to look back over your shoulder at the hole and the water and make a promise to give it another try tomorrow.

The Harbor Course, which Fazio built in 1985, is cut in and out of Morgan Creek and the Intracoastal Waterway. Jumping from one island to another, the course features water on twelve holes. The opening three holes will put a dent in your ball supply if you can't keep it out of the water on the left. Make it through that par-5, par-4, par-3 stretch with any degree of success and you'll have enough confidence to get you through to the fourteenth hole, a 492-yard par-5 framed by a thin waterway on the left and a large pond near the green on the right. Make birdie there and you've got much drier territory to navigate on the way home.

Pot bunkers (above, left), strategically placed palmetto trees (above, right), and rolling fairways that can push the ball into undesirable spots in the rough (right) are among the Tom Fazio creations that make the Links and Bay courses worth an extended stay at Wild Dunes.

Sea Island Resort
Sea Island, Georgia

Sea Island Resort
Tel.: (800) SEAISLAND
Fax: (912) 638-5159
www.seaisland.com

Designer: **Walter Travis/Dick Wilson (Plantation Course); H. S. Colt and C. S. Alison (Seaside Course); Joe Lee (Retreat Course, formerly the St. Simons Course)**

Date opened: **1927, with 1998 redesign by Rees Jones (Plantation); 1920s, with 1999 redesign by Tom Fazio (Seaside); 1920s, with 2001 redesign by Davis Love III (Retreat)**

Number of holes: **54**

Fees: **$145–$225**

Yardage/par: **7,058 yards, par-72 (Plantation); 6,745 yards, par-70 (Seaside); 7,106 yards, par-72 (Retreat)**

Rating/slope: **73.9/135 (Plantation); 73.2/131 (Seaside); 73.9/135 (Retreat)**

Pro shop: **High-end apparel bearing the Sea Island crest, plus a variety of equipment**

Golf instruction: **For individual or group sessions, at Sea Island Schools Golf Learning Center, headed by Jack Lumpkin, Davis Love III's coach**

Driving range/putting green: **300-yard deep range, with target greens, as well as practice bunker areas and large putting green**

Rentals: **Clubs (club testing available at learning center)**

Many resorts boast of their world-famous this or otherworldly that. Precious few can say the world is coming to them. Sea Island, celebrating its seventy-fifth year as one of America's preeminent resorts, is hosting the thirtieth annual G-8 Summit, from June 8 to 10, 2004. While the leaders of Canada, France, Germany, Italy, Japan, Russia, the United Kingdom, and the United States will be discussing some serious geopolitical issues, chances are they will all be Jonesin' for a tee time. Speaking of the Joneses, Bill Jones III, an innkeeper in the truest sense of the word and fourth-generation chairman and CEO of Sea Island, is ushering in a remarkable new era for the resort. As part of the $200-million, three-stage, five-year plan, Jones has overseen the demolition of the famed Cloister hotel; in its place will be an updated, amenity-laden modern structure that will no doubt retain the spirit of the hotel that stood for the previous seventy-five years. In addition to the hotel, there are cottages and The Lodge at Sea Island.

The Plantation, Seaside, and Retreat courses, all redesigns of early twentieth-century architects' works, were created by Rees Jones, Tom Fazio, and Davis Love III, respectively. The courses highlight tradition and history, and are distinct from one another, giving visitors the chance to test themselves against the courses and the elements found on this island situated between the Atlantic Ocean and the Black Banks River. This is the kind of place for which superlatives were invented and, ultimately, no words do it justice until you see it for yourself.

AS THE FIRST PHASE of Sea Island Resort's five-year renovation plan unfolds in 2004, the new hotel will be finished. The hotel will be full of architectural elements (mantelpieces, wood trim, etc.) from the Cloister Hotel that stood before it. There will also be two new river houses on the Black Banks for eating and relaxing. Renovations won't cause any interruption in spa and fitness center activities.

The fitness center continues to offer more than a dozen different programs, including tai chi on the beach, cardio-kickboxing, and fairway flexibility. Taking care of body and mind in the spa includes the Royal Rose Body Treatment. A product of the Aromatherapy Associates of London, it offers the most fragrant organic Damascan roses on the planet. The market value of essential oil of rose is ranked higher than gold, since it takes more than two thousand roses to make just one ounce. If you'd rather play in the mud, you can try the Thalasomineral Kur remineralizing treatment from the famous thermal Sarvar Springs of Hungary. The mud at the bottom of the ninety-degree lake is more than twenty thousand years old and is detoxifying and rejuvenating when used as a mask.

When you just can't choose among the other twenty or so spa options, set sail from the yacht club (beginning, intermediate, or skilled courses are available), take to the stables for a horseback ride on the beach, or test your eye at the shooting school, where you will find skeet, trap, and sporting shooting.

THE GOLF COURSES have gotten a lot of attention since the Rees Jones era of redesign at Sea Island. His course is actually a combination of what had been two separate nines, Walter Travis's Plantation and Dick Wilson's Retreat. Jones added and widened water hazards on this parkland layout with ocean views, flipped certain holes, and redirected the Retreat holes from outward to homeward, creating a new look and feel that makes for a better, more cohesive course. Jones and crew built out the bunkers in many varied forms, raising fairways and greens, and adding mounding to the sides of the fairways (some of which help poorly struck balls, some of which hurt poorly struck balls).

Tom Fazio combined the Marshside and Seaside nines when he redid the courses in 1999. He and his crew did some pretty extensive surgery, enlarging the greens and making them convex, expanding the tees, reshaping the fairways, and adding plenty of natural wild vegetation, the kind of vegetation you hate when you're having a bad day on the course. What remained of the original nines by H. S. Colt and C. S. Alison was replaced and polished. It'll also stay in your mind's eye as the best course on the resort grounds. A welcome addition to any golf resort, walking is allowed with a mandatory caddie program making the journey that much better.

Sea Island bought the St. Simons Island Club, just up the road from the resort, in 2000. Jones then hired longtime Sea Island touring pro Davis Love III and his brother, Mark, for a redesign. The old Joe Lee course was a typical, flat, low-country layout, and it's one of the three redesigns that didn't involve adding millions of cubic yards of dirt. Love did lengthen it, which is not surprising—he is, after all, one of the tour's big hitters. Love has also added a little excitement to what was once a sleepy layout, winding the course through the woods and bringing water into play.

Sea Island provides a sense of welcome relaxation, whether you want to sit beneath a canopy of massive oaks (far left), tee up on the spectacular courses (left and above, left), or check out some of the beautiful homes during a walk or run along the long stretch of beach (above, right).

Grand Cypress Resort
Orlando, Florida

Grand Cypress Resort
One North Jacaranda
Orlando, FL 32836
Tel.: (407) 239-4700
or (877) 330-7377
Fax: (407) 239-1969
www.grandcypress.com

Designer: **Jack Nicklaus**

Date opened: **1984 (North and South Courses); 1986 (East Course);
1988 (New Course)**

Number of holes: **45, but Nicklaus also designed the 9-hole Pitch 'n' Putt
course around Lake Windsong that features 37- to 90-yard holes**

Fees: **$175–$225**

Yardage/par: **6,955 yards, par-72 (East/North); 6,983 yards,
par-72 (North/South); 6,896 yards, par-72 (South/East);
6,773 yards, par-72 (New)**

Rating/slope: **75/139 (East/North); 75.1/137 (North/South);
74.7/138 (South/East); 72.2/122 (New)**

Pro shop: **Great selection of golf apparel, equipment, and
casual clothes**

Golf instruction: **For individual or group sessions, the Grand Cypress
Academy of Golf is one of the top twenty-five in the United States**

Driving range/putting green: **The range is what you would expect from a
top-notch school—huge, with practice bunkers to work on your sand
game; the large putting green is level at one end and tiered at the
other for effective practice on straight and big-breaking putts**

Rentals: **Clubs**

It might be a small world after all, but that doesn't mean that you'd want to spend all your time in Mickey's town, with rooms, sandwiches, drinks, and waiters bearing the names and likenesses of Mr. Mouse and all of his pals. Featuring an eighteen-story atrium and the chatter of parrots and macaws perched throughout the lobby, the Grand Cypress Resort, part of the Hyatt Regency, represents a two-pronged oasis of understatement with its 750 rooms and seventy-four suites in the shadow of Epcot Center. There are also seventy-five one- to four-bedroom villas a few miles away, within walking distance of the forty-five-hole golf course designed by Jack Nicklaus. In addition, the resort offers a world-class practice and teaching facility and a variety of other activities without a single Happy Meal merchandising angle.

The resort also carries with it a certain air of elegance since guests staying at the villas will likely be privy to many sightings of people sauntering, trotting, or galloping about the grounds: the Grand Cypress Equestrian Center is home to a variety of teaching and training facilities for hardcore riders or visitors out to revisit their childhood Lone Ranger longings. So, for the city slicker or experienced horse-lover, the bogey-shooter or scratch player, or even the Disney fan who likes to get away from the mayhem at the end of the day, Grand Cypress has plenty of options to keep its guests busy.

THE GRAND CYPRESS RESORT's full fitness center, located at the Hyatt Regency, provides a variety of cardiovascular and strength-training equipment, as well as personal training sessions. The resort offers in-room spa sessions featuring a variety of massage treatments, tai chi or yoga classes, and even an aromatherapy cellulite body wrap. A half-acre outdoor pool just off the fitness center features twelve waterfalls, two water slides, whirlpools, and live entertainment. The twenty-one-acre Lake Windsong is a perfect peaceful complement, home to a variety of nature hiking trails, running paths, and horse trails.

Dining options are, of course, plentiful, and include fine dining at the Black Swan or La Coquina restaurants. More casual diners will find ribs, steaks, and seafood at Hemingways or the White Horse Saloon, which provide a Key West and western vibe, respectively. Of course, after a long day of working on your drives or putting a pony through its paces on the steeplechase course, you might be more inclined to order room service and listen to the gentle breeze blow through the property.

IT'S ALL JACK, ALL THE TIME at Grand Cypress, but these three nine-hole tracks and their possible permutations give you the chance to play three difficult courses that get a bit more familiar each time around. The North and South nines have matured into humps, bumps, hillocks, and grassy knolls. While the layouts certainly don't feel native to the flat terrain indigenous to the greater Orlando area, they do feature generous landing areas from the tee. The greens are tiny; if you don't possess Nicklausian accuracy with your irons, spend a lot of pre-round practice on bunker play and short-game solutions.

The East nine has a sort of Pinehurst feel as it runs through forests of scrub pines and oak trees. The East and North nines make the best marriage of penal and pleasant design. But while the original twenty-seven holes are the most challenging, the eighteen-hole New Course, designed with more than a little inspiration from St. Andrews's Old Course, is the most fun you'll have on the Grand Cypress courses. The course received a lot of publicity when it opened in 1988 and does its level best to make you feel that you're as far from ninety-degree days as possible. From the replica starter's shack to the football-field-wide first and eighteenth fairways, you can have a blast playing this wind-whipped stretch of Florida land. Were it not for the Sunshine State's eponymous and abundant commodity, you could almost imagine yourself in the "auld grey toon." There are seven double greens; pot bunkers you can get lost in; abundant opportunities for bump-and-run shots; and even a passable attempt to recreate the storied Road Hole.

Left: There's plenty of water to get your attention on the resort's North, South, and East courses. Above: The comfortable fairway villas at Grand Cypress allow you to watch play go by as you prepare for your own round or relive good shots.

Ponte Vedra Inn & Club
Ponte Vedra, Florida

Ponte Vedra Inn & Club
200 Ponte Vedra Boulevard
Ponte Vedra Beach, FL 32082
Tel.: **(800) 234-7842**
Fax: **(904) 285-2111**
www.pvresorts.com

Designer: **Herbert Bertram Strong, with renovation by Bobby Weed (Ocean Course); Robert Trent Jones, Sr., with renovation by Joe Lee (Lagoon Course)**

Date opened: **1928 (Ocean); 1961 (Lagoon)**

Number of holes: **36**

Fees: **$110–$185**

Yardage/par: **6,871 yards, par-72 (Ocean); 5,574 yards, par-70 (Lagoon)**

Rating/slope: **73.3/138 (Ocean); 67.3/116 (Lagoon)**

Pro shop: **Variety of shops open throughout the resort, selling equipment and golf and casual apparel**

Golf instruction: **For individual or group sessions; instructors work with golfers of all playing levels, providing video analysis and comparison with the world's top players**

Driving range/putting green: **Practice facility includes range, putting green, chipping green, and sand bunker area**

Rentals: **Clubs**

Were it not for the cancellation of the 1939 Ryder Cup as tensions escalated in Europe, the entire world would be in love with the Ponte Vedra Inn & Club. Had the matches been played here, golfers all over would have read about the world's first island green (not the one built almost fifty years later up the road at the TPC Sawgrass), and the ninth hole of the Ocean Course, a 146-yard par-3—the first place that golfers had to swallow hard and hit a shot that left nothing but water from tee to green. Sixty-five years later, the three-hundred-acre resort has 221 rooms at the Inn, and another sixty-six oceanfront rooms and suites at its Lodge & Club facility. Ponte Vedra Inn has earned high praise from *Golf Digest* as one of the seventy-five best resorts in the nation and has reached prestigious AAA four-diamond status.

Ponte Vedra, which has become one of Florida's top golf destinations, lies one half-hour south of Jacksonville. It began as a mining town, rich in ilmenite and zirconium, once vital ingredients for the making of steel. As soon as executives from the mining companies breathed the fresh air and swam the vast beaches, they decided that Ponte Vedra would also be a great place to bring their families, and a resort was born.

The Ocean and Lagoon courses are opposite each other. The Ocean Course is wide and long, running over and around dunes and water through the large undulating greens. The short and tight Lagoon Course is a tricky layout, where position is more important than length off the tee.

THE PONTE VEDRA INN & CLUB, which features white-washed stucco and Spanish architecture, exudes an old-world charm. Classic pictures adorn the walls inside, where exposed beams run the length of the large rooms. High tea is served each afternoon in the lobby. Generations of families come back year after year to support the resort, so the resort has supported them—and anyone else smart enough to try it out. A $65-million renovation and upgrade has been underway since 1998, and it is evident throughout. The Island House, opened at the beginning of 2004, provides twenty-eight rooms and suites overlooking the ninth hole's island green and puts guests right in the heart of the action.

Fly-fishing enthusiasts can take to the Intracoastal Waterway for speckled trout, crappies, and snook. It is a perfect way to concentrate on something other than a five-foot putt with three feet of break. For those not interested in waders, hooks, or reels, the new 8,000-square-foot oceanfront gym gives you plenty of motivation to work out while enjoying the resort's fifteen miles of beachfront access. If you don't want to stay in the Inn you could always bunk in the aforementioned Lodge & Club, which features luxury oceanfront restaurants available to anyone staying at the resort.

In the spa, you can relax in the private garden room, complete with waterfall and Jacuzzi, or you can opt for the Sea Mud Pack, Salt Rub, or Body Polish treatments. You might want to try the Milk and Honey Rehydrating Treatment as well, but the most unusual treatment could be the Aroma/Algae Purification Treatment, combining thalasso, algae, and aromatherapy elements. The skin emerges looking smoother, firmer, and more evenly structured. Ideal results are achieved with a series of six to ten treatments. Looks like you'll just have to stay those extra days.

THE OCEAN COURSE, originally designed in 1928 by Herbert Bertram Strong with the help of a crew of workers and one hundred mules dredging lagoons to get enough mud and sand to build mounds, is simply a blast to play. There are doglegs around water, split fairways with go-for-broke options on par-5s. The course has been renovated by Robert Trent Jones Sr. (1947) and Bobby Weed (1998). It has character, and the aforementioned island hole is a treat for historical purposes. The greens are huge, slick, and tricky. The wind is always exerting its influence, often dying behind a dune or freshening through a stand of palm trees. If you survive the par-4 seventeenth, which features an elevated green and fairway bunkers that make getting near said green nearly impossible, it's all downhill from there. The elevated tee on the eighteenth provides an all-encompassing view of the resort, the Atlantic Ocean, and the hole cut into the curvy green. A birdie will go a long way toward improving your demeanor.

While it is difficult to ever read any golf literature without seeing the adjective "sporty" attached to short courses, the Lagoon Course (designed by Robert Trent Jones Sr. in 1961 and redone by Joe Lee in 1978) is a target-oriented treat. Obviously, the driver doesn't come out to play too often, but a well-placed tee shot can lead to a well-placed approach. However, the tiny greens are difficult to read and even more difficult to putt (as is only fitting on a short course). There are bodies of water in play on eleven holes, and while you would think that being on the inland course would spare you from the local gusts, you're wrong. In addition, scrub pines, large oaks, and palm trees serve as capable protection against birdie for the course.

Clockwise, from bottom left: Features of the Ponte Vedra Inn & Club include rustic charm; exposed beams; Spanish-inspired architecture; and miles of undeveloped beachfront property, perfect for post-golf activities.

The Broadmoor
Colorado Springs, Colorado

The Broadmoor
One Lake Avenue
Colorado Springs, CO 80906
Tel.: (800) 634-7711
or (719) 577-5775
Fax: (719) 577-5738
www.broadmoor.com

Designer: **Donald Ross (East Course); Robert Trent Jones Sr. (West Course); Ed Seay (Mountain Course)**

Date opened: **1918 (East); 1964 (West); 1976 (Mountain)**

Number of holes: **45 (nine of the Mountain Course holes are being restored)**

Fees: **$75–$165, depending on season**

Yardage/par: **7,144 yards, par-72 (East); 7,190 yards, par-72 (West); 3,103 yards, par-36 (Mountain)**

Rating/slope: **72.6/131 (East); 72.9/133 (West); under construction (Mountain)**

Pro shop: **The main clubhouse includes the pro shop; the Mountain Course has its own shop**

Golf instruction: **Individual or group sessions available**

Driving range/putting green: **Multitiered practice range with five target greens, two chipping/bunker greens, and three putting greens**

Rentals: **Clubs and shoes**

The Broadmoor couldn't have a more impeccable pedigree. The firm that created New York City's Grand Central Terminal built the hotel. Frederick Law Olmstead's firm designed the grounds. Donald Ross built the first golf course, on which Jack Nicklaus won his first major championship, the 1959 U.S. Amateur, and Robert Trent Jones Sr. built the second course.

The Broadmoor, with seven hundred rooms and suites, has existed for eighty-five years as one of the United States' preeminent resorts, once known as the "Riviera of the Rockies," a frequent destination for presidents and wealthy industrialists. Today, the 3,000-acre resort is part honest-to-goodness historical landmark and part twenty-first-century haven. With significant upgrades to the rooms, eleven restaurants, and the spa, the resort is a place where guests can enjoy a stay without ever leaving the grounds. Despite its 6,800-foot elevation, the daytime high temperatures range from fifty to eighty-two degrees over the course of a year.

If you have no other desire than to play on the courses that Donald Ross and Robert Trent Jones Sr. built, you've also come to the right place. Ross built the East Course in 1918 and Jones built the West Course in 1964. Jones was also entrusted with redoing the Ross layout. As you wander the halls of the resort, there is remarkable evidence of that era: A picture adorning the halls of the Broadmoor's West building was taken in the early 1950s, when Jones was at the resort to scout the course with his wife, Ione, and their future course architects, Robert Jr. and Rees. The two boys, roughly around twelve and ten, respectively, are flanking Candace Bergen, who was about half their age. Bergen was staying at the resort while her father, Edgar, was performing with his dummy sidekick, Charlie McCarthy.

FOR THE CONVENTIONAL RESORT-GOER, the 90,000-square-foot clubhouse provides access to the second-floor fitness center, complete with cardiovascular and strength-training equipment, classes, and personal training sessions. You can also enjoy the indoor pool, but to get the full effect, you might want to concentrate on your backstroke so you can check out the light streaming down through the stained-glass skylight. In the spa, opt for the Colorado Evergreen Body Polish, a mild exfoliating treatment with evergreen followed by lemon sage emollient. Once you smell good, you can indulge in the Harmonic Hot Stone Massage, which features a chakra-toning stone lay-out aimed at enhancing and balancing your energy field. In addition, harmonic sound waves are played to clear out negative emotional and mental energy.

Here's where the serene is replaced by the extreme: you can take a hike along the South Cheyenne Canyon, which features a 227-step stairway leading you through a path of seven waterfalls, culminating in a 181-foot drop through rock formations of Pike's Peak Granite (the 14,110-foot Pike's Peak summit is seven miles from the resort). You can also enjoy guided whitewater rafting tours down the Arkansas River. Rock climbers of all abilities can test themselves either on the sandstone rock formations of the nearby Garden of the Gods or in Cheyenne Canyon, set on an alpine forest with creeks and towering granite rock formations.

To mark your survival of challenges great or small, gather with other guests at the Tavern, opened in 1934 to celebrate the end of Prohibition. A casual eatery today, it's the place to go for prime rib and steaks cooked over a wood-burning grill, as well as live entertainment. As if to single-handedly ward off any teetotaling spirits, the resort also boasts a three-thousand-bottle wine cellar.

Donald Ross created The Broadmoor's East Course (above), which was then tweaked by Robert Trent Jones Sr. Jones liked the property so much that he built the West Course (left). In each case, the classic designs utilize elevation changes, generous fairways, and trees that frame the holes.

DONALD ROSS COMPLETED THE EAST COURSE at The Broadmoor in 1918, making it at the time the highest eighteen-hole golf course in the United States. Nicklaus's U.S. Amateur victory was just one of many championships played on the East Course; the 1995 U.S. Women's Open Championship was the most recent major event played there. The course still bears many of the Ross touches from when he cut it out of 135 acres of scrub oak and brush. Robert Trent Jones Sr. was officially hired in 1958 to design the West Course with an additional nine holes so that members and guests could still play while tournaments were being held on the East Course. At that time, Jones also began the renovations to the East Course. Six years later, he finished the second nine on the West Course. A more forgiving course, known for its wide fairways and large receptive greens, it has perennially been named one of the top American layouts.

The West Course bears the Jones trademark of wide fairways shrinking to tough approaches into elevated greens protected by water and sand. He added many doglegs to the West Course, tempting golfers emboldened by the thin air to cut off as much—and often more—than they should. Golfers can get views of Pike's Peak, Cheyenne Mountain, the resort, and downtown Colorado Springs from the rolling fairways and multilevel greens.

The Mountain Course, formerly known as the South Course, is located nearly at the base of Cheyenne Mountain. It is currently being played as a nine-holer while the nine holes that were wrecked by brutal rains three years ago are restored. Created in 1976 by Ed Seay, the guru of golf architecture for Arnold Palmer's massive golf-design company, it lies roughly a mile away from the main clubhouse. With a separate clubhouse, it offers players a series of dramatic views of Colorado Springs from tight fairways squeezed by scrub oaks. The fairways stop and start over and around ravines that cut across the property, making position, and not length, the premium.

Left: From a covered patio, Broadmoor guests can sip and snack while enjoying the fresh air and scenic vistas that you get from being 6,850 feet above sea level. Above: The marble lobby conjures up images of The Broadmoor's luxurious beginnings at the turn of the twentieth century.

The Boulders
Carefree, Arizona

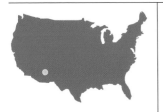

The Boulders
34631 North Tom Darlington Dr.
P.O. Box 2090
Carefree, AZ 85377
Tel.: (800) 553-1717
or (480) 488-9009
Fax: (702) 567-4777
www.wyndham.com

Designer: **Jay Morrish**

Date opened: **1969 (North, originally opened as Carefree Municipal Golf Course); 1983 (South)**

Number of holes: **36**

Fees: **$75–$230, depending on season**

Yardage/par: **6,811 yards, par-72 (North); 6,726 yards, par-72 (South)**

Rating/slope: **72.6/137 (North); 71.9/140 (South)**

Pro shop: **One of the most well appointed shops in the U.S.; women's merchandise is as plentiful as men's**

Golf instruction: **Individual or group sessions available for men and women; the Women to the Fore program is one of the premiere instruction centers for beginning women golfers**

Driving range/putting green: **Vast range and chipping, putting, and bunker areas provide plenty of room for practice**

Rentals: **Clubs and shoes**

The Boulders doesn't feel as though it was built, but rather materialized; it is one of the rare places that seems full of the spirit of the land, not born of bucketfuls of cash and a couple of local heirlooms. For fifteen years, the resort has been a safe haven for people ready to get away from the daily grind and recharge their batteries—through outdoor activities of all sorts, through spa treatment after spa treatment, or of course, by playing some golf.

For those interested in chasing that little white ball around, this is the place that could be known as Jurassic Golf. The North Course and South Course provide some of the finest, and earliest, tests of true desert golf. Famed architect Jay Morrish created two layouts that test your patience, your eye, and your nerve. Will you go in among the cacti, brush, and critters to fetch a ball? You'd be better served to drop one on the edge of the grass and not blow the calm you'll have obtained within your first couple of hours at the resort.

If you're looking for the monolithic hotel as you pull into the resort, you're in the wrong place. The colossal rock formations, remnants of the 12,000,000-year-old geological shift that ultimately led to the formation of the Grand Canyon, are creased and turned, looming in seemingly precarious positions above the 160 casitas that are shaped and colored in tones so muted they almost seem to have been here as long as the huge outcroppings. The natural and native touches, from fireplaces to Navajo blankets, imbue the resort with an enveloping calm; in fact, for all you type-A personalities who are truly serious about getting away from it all, ask the staff to remove the phone and alarm clock from your casita. While you're at it, let them hold your cell phone, pager, and Palm Pilot, too.

THE BOULDERS FEATURES CASITAS, including forty-eight suites, which are slipped into the foothills of the Sonoran Desert. Activities include basketball courts, horseback-riding trails, sailing, hot-air balloon rides, jeep tours, water skiing, or even cattle herding—à la *City Slickers*.

After a day out in the sun, it's time to hit the Golden Door Spa, an offshoot of the original in Escondido, California. The specialists here follow the tenets of the ancient honjin inns of Japan, where travelers were revitalized through a combination of massage, therapeutic baths, and refreshment. The Boulders' Golden Door encompasses 33,000-square-feet of healing rooms, specializing in Native American wraps and therapies. The movement studio provides all levels of Pilates, yoga, and tai chi classes. In addition, the grounds feature a labyrinth, where you can follow a path to tranquility inspired by ancient Hopi medicine wheels. For those looking for retail therapy, the shops at El Pedregal are just a quick hike from the main building.

The resort offers five restaurants from which to choose; most feature rough-hewn exposed beams, Mexican tile, and an open natural feel. The Latilla, which specializes in classic American fare, has a great view of a waterfall and the boulders from the main resort building. But you're in Arizona, so go for the Mexican and Southwestern fare at Cantina del Pedregal, which has been voted the creator of Phoenix's best margarita. Choose from a variety of tequilas and special flavors.

Right: Jay Morrish, one of the founding fathers of desert target golf, has created two courses at The Boulders that place a premium on accuracy—and knowing when to let a ball stay in the brush. Far right: This lagoon provides an oasis in the middle of the desert.

THE NORTH COURSE AT THE BOULDERS began as the Carefree Municipal Golf Course in 1969, when Red Lawrence somehow fashioned nine holes from the rough land. Phoenix architect Jack Snyder completed the eighteen holes by the early 1970s, but the rockslide to greatness didn't start until Jay Morrish got to work. A decade after Snyder finished the course, Morrish was commissioned to create the South Course, which he finished in 1983. At that time, he set out to refine the North Course, completed in 1985.

The North features fairways mottled with what appear to be small moguls; the undulations provide tricky shadows as the sun stretches over the course. The browns, grays, and tans of the desert territory running on either side of the lush fairways seem ominous from the tee and on approaches to the greens, and players realize that any hope for escape from the rocky land is futile. Morrish tweaked the North Course again in 1999. The back nine is particularly difficult, especially the 457-yard thirteenth hole, which features an elevated green protected by the ever-present desert "junk." The fourteenth hole makes you appreciate what desert wanderers must have felt when they saw an oasis; the 183-yard par-3 features water from tee to green and proves tempting to golfers who've been battling for a few hours in the desert heat. The 427-yard, dogleg-left closing hole lets you bite a bit off the corner, but fairway bunkers and a little water along the left side near the green make players tentative on their way into the flag.

The South Course is a dramatic layout that gets a lion's share of the publicity. The first hole, a 447-yard par-4, makes position a must—not just for accuracy but also for distance since two stacks of huge boulders narrow the fairway at 110 yards out. The green fronts a massive pile of rocks. Airmail a shot over the green and you'll see a desert chain reaction: ball hits rocks, ball ricochets off rocks into cactus—scaring rabbits, birds, snakes, and any other creatures resting in the shade. The par-5 fifth leads you right up to the base of the signature "Boulder Pile," which makes for a great photo opportunity.

Clockwise, from top left: The casitas provide a natural haven set in and around the prehistoric remnants that give the resort its name; once inside, the rooms are full of details that give every guest a sense of being transported to another time; when the sun goes down, a fireplace takes the chill out of the air; even the pool feels like a swimming hole that developed out of the rock outcroppings.

Four Seasons Resort Scottsdale at Troon North
Scottsdale, Arizona

**Four Seasons Resort Scottsdale
at Troon North**
10600 East Crescent Moon Drive
Scottsdale, AZ 85262
Tel.: (480) 515-5700
Fax: (480) 515-5599
www.fourseasons.com/scottsdale

Designer: **Tom Weiskopf and Jay Morrish (Monument Course);**
Tom Weiskopf (Pinnacle Course)

Date opened: **1990 (Monument); 1995 (Pinnacle)**

Number of holes: **36**

Fees: **$240–$275**

Yardage/par: **7,028 yards, par-72 (Monument); 7,028 yards, par-73
(Pinnacle)**

Rating/slope: **73.3/147 (Monument); 73.4/147 (Pinnacle)**

Pro shop: **Ultra-swank clothes and equipment**

Golf instruction: **For individual or group sessions**

Driving range/putting green: **Driving range is spacious and putting
green is ample**

Rentals: **Clubs**

When Tom Weiskopf and Jay Morrish unveiled Troon North's Monument Course, people were stunned. They were stunned at the beauty that each element together created and the vision that these two shared in taking long strips of green and inserting them between even bigger strips of sand and rock—somehow creating a course that was daunting and inviting at the same time. As more people played Monument Course, more began to rave about it. By the time Weiskopf had taken the mantle to build Pinnacle Course five years later, there were plenty of people building homes around these courses, making a commitment to desert lifestyle and golf.

Shortly after the Pinnacle went up, the Four Seasons announced a plan to build in Scottsdale. The result is the sort of property the hotel chain is so skilled at creating, the natural-looking architecture integrated with the beautiful surroundings. From the 210-room hotel, guests get views of Pinnacle Peak, perfectly framed out of their luxury casita's patio door. The hotel lies just two miles from Troon North. A block of priority Troon North tee times is set aside each day for Four Seasons guests.

IF YOU OPT FOR ONE of the twenty-two casita suites at the Four Seasons, you get your own private soaking pool in which to cool down from those warm Scottsdale afternoons (and mornings, for that matter). The suites also come with a telescope, giving you the chance to gaze into the starry Arizona desert sky or at the twinkling Phoenix skyline.

The Acacia steakhouse provides an open-air setting from which to marvel at the changing colors of the Sonoran Desert as the sun begins its descent in the west. Choose from prime cuts of beef, fresh seafood, and seasonal specialties served in an intimate Southwestern setting. The casual Crescent Moon is a lively Italian bistro that features an open kitchen for diners to watch the nightly action. Suaro Blossom is the perfect sunrise-to-sunset option for a quick bite or a drink by the pool.

Said pool is a 6,000-square-foot oasis spilling onto a second level that features a whirlpool at one end for the grown-ups. There is no shortage of outdoor activities, including hot-air balloon rides above the desert, jeep tours, hiking and horseback-riding trails through Pinnacle Peak Park, and rock-climbing for the ambitious sorts. Of course, there is always the typical Four Seasons pampering to be doled out, with massages and skin treatments containing desert secrets certain to soothe frayed nerves and loosen tired muscles.

Clockwise, from above: Tom Weiskopf and Jay Morrish built the Monument Course at Troon North (shown here), which was followed by Weiskopf's solo job, the Pinnacle Course; the resort provides the details for the desert experience, from mountain-view rooms to the swimming pool, and even the howls of los lobos as the moon rises.

IF THIS IS YOUR FIRST VISIT to desert golf, Monument is the perfect indoctrination. The course Weiskopf and Morrish created is even more spectacular today, after almost fifteen years of maturation. Don't be frightened by the brown edges of the desert seemingly squeezing the fairway—an optical illusion that makes the fairways look even skinnier than they actually are. If anything, try to use it to your advantage by focusing solely on the spot you want to land the ball. Monument is a challenge, to be sure, but it is also a blast to play. The desert frequently comes into question, but the course is not a target course since there is margin for error on shots. Your tee shot on the fourteenth, however, is a test since you need to carry it across a dry desert expanse. While you are worrying about carry, you also have to worry about placement;

the long, slender green is set at a diagonal and requires an approach from the right side of the fairway.

Weiskopf's solo work on Pinnacle is a good companion course to the 1990 design. He laid this course around granite boulders and built significant elevation changes, but Pinnacle's fairways are tighter, leaving even more treacherous carries over desert landing areas. The eighteenth, the course's signature hole, is a 407-yard, par-4 and provides an outstanding view of Pinnacle Peak in the background.

Clockwise, from above: From the tee of the sixth hole of the Pinnacle Course, the green stretches of fairway look too skinny as the desert terrain squeezes it from either side; a sunset round among the cacti in the late afternoon is a good way to beat the heat; at least the huge greens of Pinnacle give players the chance to make a long birdie putt.

La Quinta Resort & Club
La Quinta, California

La Quinta Resort & Club
49–499 Eisenhower Drive
La Quinta, CA 92253
Tel.: (800) 598-3828
Fax: (760) 564-5768
www.laquintaresort.com

Designer: **Pete Dye (Mountain, Dunes, and PGA West TPC Stadium courses); Jack Nicklaus (PGA West Jack Nicklaus Course); Greg Norman (PGA West Greg Norman Course)**

Date opened: **1980 (Mountain); 1981 (Dunes); 1986 (PGA West TPC); 1987 (PGA West Jack Nicklaus); 1999 (PGA West Greg Norman)**

Number of holes: **90, but rounds at the private Citrus Course and La Quinta Country Clubs can also be arranged**

Fees: **$150–$275**

Yardage/par: **6,756 yards, par-72 (Mountain); 6,747 yards, par-72 (Dunes); 7,261 yards, par-72 (PGA West TPC); 7,126 yards, par-72 (PGA West Jack Nicklaus); 7,156 yards, par-72 (PGA West Greg Norman)**

Rating/slope: **74.1/140 (Mountain); 73.1/137 (Dunes); 75.9/150 (PGA West TPC); 74.7/139 (PGA West Jack Nicklaus); 73.1/137 (PGA West Greg Norman)**

Pro shop: **There is nothing that you can't buy at this resort, whether it's at the pro shop, the boutiques, or the branded stores by golf favorites (Cutter & Buck, Tommy Bahama)**

Golf instruction: **Available for individual or group sessions, and expert instruction available at Jim McLean Golf Academy and the Dave Pelz Short Game School**

Driving range/putting green: **With five courses from which to choose, if you can't find the right range you might want to take up tennis (which is well represented at La Quinta)**

Rentals: **Clubs**

Roughly two hours east of Los Angeles, this resort was opened in 1926 and quickly became a getaway for the fabulous people of film. Frank Capra wrote the screenplay for *It Happened One Night* here, won a slew of Academy Awards for it, and never wrote a screenplay anywhere else. Katharine Hepburn, Spencer Tracy, Doris Day, Bette Davis, Errol Flynn, Frank Sinatra, and Bob Hope are just some of the celebrities that have turned this once-abandoned desert into a swinging place to play.

Swing is now the operative word here, where roughly ninety courses (many private and near-impossible to visit with your sticks) have sprung up. At La Quinta, you can choose from courses designed by Pete Dye, Jack Nicklaus, and Greg Norman. The resort offers stunning juxtaposition of long strips of green, water, and sand surrounded by mountains that seem to change colors with each movement of the sun. A word of warning: The greens are harder to read than Nathaniel Hawthorne. The only thing harder than making par is figuring out just what else you're going to do each day. If you're concerned about missing a round due to weather, there are roughly fifteen rainy days each year in the Coachella Valley region. But there is one drawback: you might need a sweater on a winter evening.

GIVEN ITS CELLULOID CONNECTIONS, staying at La Quinta makes you feel as though you're starring in *Lifestyles of the Rich and Famous*. The eight hundred casitas (loosely translated here as "swank cottages") are spread out over the property, which instills a sense of privacy. With forty-two pools scattered about, all the golf you could want, twenty-three tennis courts, amazing spa and fitness centers, and an Olympic-sized swimming pool, you can walk around and find out just how eighty million dollars in newly completed renovations was spent.

The deluxe casitas are broken down into sixteen categories; accommodations range from "Man, this is great" to "I'm not leaving. Seriously, I'm not."

The dining options are equally amazing. The casual Mexican restaurant, Adobe Grill, is home to strolling mariachis, flowing margaritas, and guacamole made tableside. Azur by Le Bernardin, however, is a completely different experience; this restaurant once again pairs restaurateur Maguy Le Coze and chef Eric Ripert, the geniuses behind the internationally acclaimed New York City restaurant Le Bernardin. There are plenty of elements from the New York menu and not a single misstep, proving the skill of Le Coze and Ripert at not only making another restaurant work, but also finding the best locale to shake off the east coast winter blues.

Spa treatments include a Just-for-Him plan that offers a deep-cleansing facial, neck and shoulders massage, and seminar on proper shaving techniques. During the Champagne Revitalization Facial you are scrubbed with an extract of champagne yeast, which should leave you feeling bubbly. In addition there are twenty-four massage rooms in which you can get your tired or tight muscles loosened, the four open-air celestial showers let you get back to nature, and the garden fireplace is the perfect place to relax after a long day on the course—or in the spa.

Clockwise, from far left: After challenging yourself with Pete Dye's too-much-water-for-a-desert-course spectacular TPC West, you can soothe frayed nerves with either a soak in the private tub or one of the many communal pools.

THERE'S NO TELLING WHY Pete Dye was whistling a happy tune in 1980, but he must have built the Dunes Course at La Quinta with a smile on his face. Sure, the railroad ties are there, the water and nasty vegetation gobble any balls in their midst, and the undulating greens make three-putts commonplace. But if you take a deep breath—and play from the appropriate tees to the correct side of the fairways and greens—you can manage your way to a good score.

When Dye returned six years later, he made sure nobody thought he'd gone soft. The TPC Stadium Course is a Dye masterpiece, as difficult and nuanced as any of his layouts. The sadistic 75.9 rating/150 slope is enough to give you a twisted ankle or something that can be soothed at the spa, but you persevere. You split the generous fairways, build up your confidence, and then get stuck in a deep pot bunker, dunk a couple in the drink, and accept your fate. Dye got you, but you don't mind because it was a glorious mugging that you'll talk about for years.

The Nicklaus and Norman courses are similar to the Dye courses—playable if you don't try to bite off more than you can chew. Want to play from the tips even though you're a twenty-three handicap? Fine, but pack a couple of dozen balls and give yourself plenty of time to complete the task.

The Arnold Palmer Course, on which the final two rounds of the Bob Hope Chrysler Classic is played, is a scenic, challenging, private course. If you can pull a couple of strings to get an invite from a member, do it. The only other shot you have to play here is if you come to the desert in the summer, when absolutely no sane person will be on the course.

Right, top and bottom: Individual casitas provide plenty of windows and doors that open into courtyards perfect for a quiet breakfast or private time in the sun. Far right: The eighteenth hole of La Quinta's Dunes Course.

Grand Wailea Resort Hotel & Spa
Maui, Hawaii

Grand Wailea Resort Hotel & Spa
3850 Wailea Alanui
Wailea, Maui, HI 96753
Tel.: (808) 875-1234
Fax: (808) 879-4077
www.grandwailea.com

Designer: **Jack Snyder (Blue Course); Robert Trent Jones Jr. (Emerald and Gold Courses)**

Date opened: **1972 (Blue); 1994 (Emerald and Gold)**

Number of holes: **54**

Fees: **$120–$135**

Yardage/par: **6,758 yards, par-72 (Blue); 6,825 yards, par-72 (Emerald); 7,078 yards, par-72 (Gold)**

Rating/slope: **71.6/130 (Blue); 71.7/130 (Emerald); 73/139 (Gold)**

Pro shop: **Full of hats (you must protect yourself from the Hawaiian sun), logoed wear, and tropical casual après-golf clothes**

Golf instruction: **For individual or group sessions, just contact the pro shop**

Driving range/putting green: **The range is perfectly fine, but once you get your swing groove there, head for the putting greens because Hawaii's greens can be tricky**

Rentals: **Clubs**

It's just another day in paradise at the Grand Wailea Resort, where there are fifty-four holes of spectacular golf on one side of the road and a fabulous hotel and beach on the other. Built in 1991, the Grand Wailea is committed to providing a more natural feel, integrating itself with its setting and its culture. There are 780 luxurious rooms, including fifty-two suites, available in a variety of sizes, amenities, and views and the dining options feature award-winning cuisine. The resort is set upon forty oceanfront acres in the southwest corner of Maui. The golf courses include the Blue Course, known as The Grand Lady of Wailea, which was the first built on the island, in 1972, and Robert Trent Jones Jr.'s Emerald and Gold courses, which offer spectacular views of the ocean and the surrounding areas.

A short distance from the Wailea Golf Club, the Grand Wailea concierge can arrange transportation to the golf course of your choice. There are a variety of fun touches, including several pools, the Grotto Bar (a swim-up bar), and the Botero Gallery Bar (a lobby lounge full of sculptures by the Colombian artist Fernando Botero). The details make for a good vacation, especially one on unfamiliar shores, and the Grand Wailea makes it easy to sit back and enjoy Maui.

THE GRAND WAILEA IS THE PLACE for the active guest. There is parasailing, snorkeling, scuba diving, deep-sea fishing, hiking, horseback riding, kayaking, and off-road jeep tours. You can even take a ride to Haleakala, the world's largest dormant volcano. If you can't go a day without a structured workout, the fitness room gives you cardiovascular and weight-training options. You can also take stress management classes or open yourself up for a spiritual and intuitive consultation. Then again, the Boxing for Fitness class must count for stress-management credits.

In the Grande Spa, try the Coconut Euphoria treatment or the Hawaiian Kava (Awa) Bath. The latter entails a massage with a jojoba, macadamia, and kukui nut lotion and grapefruit and bearberry extract, sounding more like a dessert than a skin treatment. In fact it sounds so good, you might find yourself in the mood for lunch at Bistro Molokini, the outdoor spot perfect for staring off at the ocean while you pick through your salad. For dinner there is Humuhumunukunukuapua'a, a romantic thatched-hut Polynesian eatery that floats on a saltwater lagoon while fish swim obliviously by. The restaurant is named after the state fish, which is not on the menu.

JACK SNYDER'S BLUE COURSE at Grand Wailea, the first on Maui, is now more than thirty years old, and its wide fairways let you meander through the resort and the beautiful homes and condominiums. The Blue's seventy-four bunkers and four lakes provide a fun challenge as you try to keep your ball on the straight and not so narrow.

Robert Trent Jones Jr.'s Emerald and Gold courses, are celebrating their tenth birthdays in 2004, and are testaments to the wonders Trent Jones Jr. can do with seaside properties. The ups and downs, twists and turns in the Emerald Course might make you a bit jumpy, but always check wind and elevation, and aim for the fat part of the green to avoid the tricky green-side bunkers. Because Jones was very generous with the huge putting surfaces, shots that would otherwise miss smaller greens give you a chance to make some putts and score better.

The double green that plays to the tenth and seventeenth holes isn't a gimmick; it's a unique element that also succeeds in bringing you back to a spot that affords excellent views of the surroundings. On the 553-yard par-5 home hole, stop for a moment at the tee and check out the view of Haleakala. If you're feeling ambitious one morning, you can even get up early—really early—and climb to the top of the 10,023-foot tall crater to catch the most amazing sunrise you've ever seen. Then again, you could have a leisurely breakfast and go back over to the Emerald Course.

The Emerald and Gold courses, designed by Robert Trent Jones Jr., provide generous fairways, huge greens, and amazing views of the Pacific Ocean and still-active Haleakala Volcano. Many of the rooms provide ocean views and sliding doors that guests keep open to savor the scent of the native plumeria.

Hyatt Regency Kauai Resort and Spa
Koloa, Hawaii

Hyatt Regency Kauai
Resort and Spa
1571 Poipu Road
Koloa, HI 96756
Tel.: (808) 742-1234
Fax: (808) 742-1557
www.kauai.hyatt.com

Designer: **Robert Trent Jones Jr.**

Date opened: **1991**

Number of holes: **18**

Fees: **$145**

Yardage/par: **6,959 yards, par-72 to 5,241 yards, par-72**

Rating/slope: **73.4/132 to 70.9/121**

Pro shop: **Regularly counted as one of the top one hundred golf shops in the nation, offering a diverse selection of hard-goods, logoed gear, and island/casual clothes**

Golf instruction: **For individual or group sessions**

Driving range/putting green: **Solid range with practice targets and short-game area, practice greens almost as fast as those on the course**

Rentals: **Clubs and balls**

At once breathtaking and self-deprecating, the Hyatt Kauai Resort and Spa is precisely what going somewhere different is all about. From the minute you arrive, you feel as though you're in another land. Walking through the thirty-foot-tall front entranceway, looking through the other high-ceilinged lobby past the grounds and pool and out onto the Pacific, you're filled with an instant sense of calm and the feeling that this place hasn't changed much from its roots. The doorways and wood accents are made of native Koa wood, which looks two shades darker than oak. The touches here, especially fresh off a multimillion-dollar renovation, are details that distinguish the hotel from the others on the island.

One funny personal story that will likely get me in trouble: After playing a round of golf, I was meeting my wife, Paula, for lunch. She'd spent the morning on the beach and was visibly shaken when she showed up at the restaurant. Paula eventually asked the other people at the table, who were lifelong residents of the island, why the "dead" seals were allowed to remain on the beach, roped off by yellow tape. Ten minutes later, after the laughter had subsided only a little bit, they explained that monk seals are endangered species, so when they beach themselves after a big meal the resort ropes off the area to keep them protected from curious visitors. The discussion to me is at the heart of why this is the best resort in Kauai: Like the story, the resort is able to embrace its Hawaiian roots, laugh at the silly, and pay homage to the past.

NATIVE FLOWERS, most noticeably the plumeria, lend a sweet air to the Hyatt Regency Kauai as you linger over breakfast, watching humpback whales come up for air and do a belly flop for your benefit. You rarely go away disappointed. All 602 rooms offer a variety of views—either of the ocean, the lagoon, or the Haupu Mountains. The Dock is the perfect poolside lunch/cocktail spot, while Tidepools is a contemporary Hawaiian restaurant assembled in a lovely collection of outdoor *hale pili* (thatched huts) nestled among waterfalls and koi ponds.

The recently renovated 28,000-square-foot spa solidifies a commitment to fitness and wellness. Called the ANARA (A New Age Restorative Approach) Spa, it includes open-air native treatments and showers in a waterfall-like lava rock setting. Before you take your Lomi-Lomi Massage, you will be greeted with a Hawaiian chant from your masseuse. The technique with this massage entails more vigorous and rhythmic strokes; the professionals also use their elbows and forearms to work their magic on those knots that are hard to loosen. The Thai Massage is a combination of massage, stretching, and manipulation. The focus here is on pressure points, energy lines, and the basic body forces to aid ease of movement. Couples can also take an instructional massage that will help them work on each other. There is a lovely parting gift too: an instructional manual and complimentary oil selection. In addition to the services, the spa provides fitness classes and yoga instruction. Once your shakras have been aligned you might want to jump into a kayak and paddle among the fives acres of salt-water lagoons on the property, or you could just go for a freefall on the 150-foot waterslide (you have the Hyatt's approval to behave like a kid here).

FOR THE PAST TEN YEARS, the golf course at the Hyatt Regency Kauai Resort and Spa has been good enough to host the most difficult tournament in the world. The PGA Grand Slam of Golf is a two-day, silly-season tournament that is open to only those players who have won that year's major championships. For ten years, there have been no complaints about the venue.

Robert Trent Jones Jr. has the market cornered on each end of the island, and like the courses he designed at Princeville (see pages 154–57), he's given players here the chance to see the ocean from all eighteen holes. As though just seeing water isn't enough, the course also has water in play on eleven holes. The holes run around the remains of some Hawaiian *heiau*, or places of worship, and there are instances in which a golf ball that lands on a particular spot can't be retrieved because it would be an affront to the deities to set foot on the soil. The fairways on the course might be almost too generous. They are so wide that you get a false sense of security and think no matter how much you overswing, you can still keep it out of the trash. That said, the front nine plays much longer since the wind is at you almost every step of the way. And that wind is a huge help on the back nine, which is likely why Jones built a 501-yard par-4 sixteenth there. This hole can scare you all the way around the course, as it seems to jump off the scorecard at you. Once you get on the tee and see that you actually benefit from the elevated tee and tailwind, you can breath a sigh of relief and play the hole with some degree of confidence. As great as this course is, it also has one of the best perks in resort golf. After four o'clock in the afternoon, an adult and a junior (a golfer under eighteen) can go out, carrying their own bags, for just ten dollars. It's worth the late dinner reservation for such a special round.

The Hyatt Regency Kauai Resort's inland holes provide dramatic backdrops of volcanic mountains (far left, top), but its holes along the coast are among the world's most memorable (far left, bottom). The resort runs along the beach (left, top), but manmade channels run from the courtyard to the surf (left, middle and bottom).

Opulent

The advent of modern-day golf-resort development coincided with an unprecedented jump in the economy, the evolution of golf travel in the United States, and the onslaught of the Baby Boomer generation. As a result, the courses grew bigger, bolder, and more dramatic; the resorts were sleeker, shinier, and full of amenities that would appeal to the well-heeled. At these resorts, pampering is par for the course. Each has a flair for finding your soft spots and then treating them until you achieve a sense of relaxation that golfers generally only associate with the best round of their lives.

104

110

116

122

128

134

140

144

148

154

158

164

168

Nemacolin Woodlands Resort & Spa
Farmington, Pennsylvania

Nemacolin Woodlands Resort & Spa
1001 LaFayette Drive
Farmington, PA 15437
Tel.: (800) 422-2736
Fax: (724) 329-8555
www.nemacolin.com

Designer: **unnamed (Links Course); Pete Dye (Mystic Rock)**

Date opened: **1969 (Links); 1995 (Mystic Rock)**

Number of holes: **36**

Fees: **$84–$130**

Yardage/par: **6,643 yards, par-71 (Links); 6,832 yards, par-72 (Mystic Rock)**

Rating/slope: **73/131 (Links); 75/146 (Mystic Rock)**

Pro shop: **Full-line shop stocked with high-end apparel and equipment**

Golf instruction: **The 3,000-square-foot John Daly Learning Center features four hitting bays equipped with the latest electronic and video systems, a classroom, an indoor short game area including putting greens, a chipping area, practice bunkers, a club repair center, a club-fitting center, and a launch machine for club fitting**

Driving range/putting green: **Huge range and putting greens that are just as much fun as the course**

Rentals: **Clubs and shoes**

If it was anybody else, you would probably have a hard time liking a guy with a ton of dough, a fabulous golf resort, and the juice to get the PGA Tour to bring an event—the 84 Lumber Classic of Pennsylvania—to southwestern Pennsylvania. However, we're talking about Joe Hardy, owner of 84 Lumber, and it's difficult to think poorly of a regular guy who made it big, and who, for the last twenty years, has spent a lot of money turning a forty-year-old resort in the Laurel Highlands into a destination. The resort touts itself as "West Coast Attitude/East Coast Latitude," but it is also a place where Hardy apparently gets an idea and then runs with it until it's completed. Want a second course? Call Pete Dye, and Mystic Rock is born. Need some fun? Build, in no particular order, an activities center with rock-climbing wall; Mystic Mountain ski slope; the Sundial Lodge, home to the Hungry Moose Café and The Hitchin' Post Saloon; the Hummer Driving Club; and the Woodlands Outdoor World, a 50,000-square-foot haven for hunting, fishing, and camping gear. Simply put, when Joe Hardy bought the resort at auction in 1987 and started running it with his daughter, Maggie Hardy Magerko, they decided it would be a place where no one would leave unhappy.

NEMACOLIN WAS NAMED for a Delaware Indian chief who cut a path through the woods of southwestern Pennsylvania that was traversed by George Washington during the French and Indian War. In the mid-1800s, U.S. Congress declared this the first highway; today, it is known as Interstate Route 40. As the Hardys continued to cut their own path for the resort, they built Chateau LaFayette, a 124-room inn that features Lautrec, the French bistro. In 1998 they dropped fourteen million dollars on a spa renovation. A sign in the spa recounts a Chinese proverb, "Tension is who you think you should be. Relaxation is who you are." These are indeed some pretty relaxed people, and while there is no "Hardy Scrub," you can have anything from paraffin, mud, moss, seaweed, or algae applied to your body in order to exfoliate, slim, soothe, and reinvigorate yourself. In addition to the spa services, there are a number of nutritionists you can talk with to prepare yourself for the fitness room where you can try yoga, Pilates, work with a personal trainer, or just do some old-fashioned exercising on the treadmills.

Left: The Mystic Rock layout, built by Pete Dye, is home to the PGA Tour's 84 Lumber Classic. The course feels like a Jurassic excavation. Above: People who finish their work on the course can dig into some treats on the large clubhouse patio and watch other players finish their rounds.

WHEN HARDY WORKED OUT a deal with the PGA Tour to host the September event at Nemacolin each year, it was met by a lot of people with an incredulous, "Where?" That is no longer the case as Hardy's story gets out and more and more people see pictures of the Mystic Rock Course. Dye's handiwork looks a bit Jurassic, with huge boulders and massive amounts of sand and water covering the terrain. The enormous rolling greens look almost proportionate to the scale of this course. The course's wide fairways winnow to tight approaches into the greens. Pick from among the five sets of tees to find out what's right for you and you'll have an enjoyable day. One nice touch: There will be no logjam at the halfway house. You simply call your order in after your tee shot on the ninth tee. By the time you finish the hole, you hit the drive-through window at Mulligan's and keep going on the way to the tenth tee.

The Links Course, which was the first course opened at the resort in the late 1960s, is a playable layout trying to approximate the linksland experience in the middle of a Pennsylvania forest. It is no match for Mystic Rock, but if you want a break from the beast, you'll have fun.

Not that it should surprise you, but there will soon be another addition to the grounds. Construction is wrapping up on Falling Rock, a full-service pro shop and forty-two-room lodge that will feature butler service, an executive boardroom, men's and women's locker rooms, a dining room, lounge, and outdoor pool and patio. It is set to open in August 2004.

Left: Nemacolin offers clubby interiors in the locker rooms (top) and Tudor-style accommodations (bottom). Above: Dye's Mystic Rock course features his trademark use of forced carries into the greens.

Kiawah Island Golf Resort
Kiawah Island, South Carolina

Kiawah Island Golf Resort
12 Kiawah Beach Drive
Kiawah Island, SC 29455
Tel.: (800) 576-1570
Fax: (843) 768-6093
www.kiawahresort.com

Designer: **Gary Player (Cougar Point); Jack Nicklaus (Turtle Point); Tom Fazio (Osprey Point); Clyde Johnston (Oak Point); Pete Dye (Ocean Course)**

Date opened: **1976, with 1997 redesign (Cougar Point); 1981 (Turtle Point); 1988 (Osprey Point); 1989 (Oak Point); 2000 (Ocean)**

Number of holes: **90**

Fees: **$90–$245**

Yardage/par: **6,887, par-72 (Cougar Point); 7,054, par-72 (Turtle Point); 6,871, par-72 (Osprey Point); 6,759, par-72 (Oak Point); 7,296, par-72 (Ocean)**

Rating/slope: **134/73 (Cougar Point); 141/74.2 (Turtle Point); 137/72.9 (Osprey Point); 140/73.8 (Oak Point); 152/78 (Ocean)**

Pro shop: **Well-appointed, high-end equipment and apparel**

Golf instruction: **For individual or group sessions**

Driving range/putting green: **Practice range and green, chipping area**

Rentals: **Clubs**

Every conversation you have with a fellow golf traveler about Kiawah Island Golf Resort begins with an arched eyebrow, a pained expression, and a "Did the Ocean Course kill you?" To be fair, Pete Dye's brutal windblown masterpiece at the eastern end of the island just about twenty miles south of Charleston should be a focal point of any Kiawah conversation. But if you begin and end there, you've missed the boat. Tom Fazio, Jack Nicklaus, Gary Player, and Clyde Johnston built courses from 1976 through 1989 that turned a sleepy piece of property bordered by the Kiawah River and the Atlantic Ocean into a booming resort region. When Dye's design opened in 1991, just in time for one of history's most dramatic Ryder Cup competitions, the resort—and the region—captured the attention of a worldwide audience.

Since then, Kiawah Island has continued to grow into a habitat for golfers and outdoors enthusiasts. This spring, it is unveiling another addition that just might have people talking about something new and exciting that's not related to the Ocean Course.

IN THE PAST, visitors could choose their lodging options at Kiawah Island Golf Resort to be as pampered or private as they pleased. The casual but elegant 150-room Kiawah Island Inn provided a traditional hotel setting, complete with restaurants such as the Atlantic Room or the West Beach Café and Bar. Or they could move into one of the three- to six-bedroom rental homes or one- to three-bedroom villas that overlook the courses, lagoons, and tennis courts. The variety of options have always made Kiawah a favorite among active golfers and their families. The ten miles of pristine beaches are perfect for ocean-kayaking, boogie-boarding, and various boating activities; the thirty miles of bike/running paths through the saltwater marshes and wooded areas are perfect for nature tours or even a weekly scavenger hunt for families.

The year 2004, however, has ushered in yet another, more opulent option for Kiawah devotees. Opening in March, The Sanctuary at Kiawah Island will provide visitors with an oceanfront hotel with 255 guestrooms. Built in the shape of a horseshoe facing the Atlantic, the hotel will open from the lobby onto an expansive green that leads down to the beach. It will feature the decor of the British West Indies and will allow guests to indulge in fine dining and luxurious bars. The Sanctuary's rooms will have oceanfront balconies, marble showers, and five-fixture baths. In addition, the hotel will feature a nature-based luxury spa dedicated to providing high-end pampering for souls adventurous or in repose. It will offer a variety of massage, facial, and wrap treatments in its thirteen special treatment rooms. Experts in the beauty salon wait to provide finishing touches to enhance a low-key evening of relaxation. Now, what was the name of that nasty old golf course again?

Left and above: Kiawah's courses were designed by some of modern golf's top architects and player-architects. While each of the courses is unique, they all feature a successful marriage of natural landscape and golf-course treachery.

WHEN PETE DYE FINISHED Kiawah's Ocean Course in 1991, just in time for the Ryder Cup, he seemed humbled by the accomplishment. The course itself humbled some of the Ryder Cup competitors, who shed more than a few tears over the things that the winds off the Atlantic could do to their golf balls. More than a decade later, golfers from around the globe continue to make the pilgrimage to test themselves against the layout that provides plenty of space on the fairways but tightens the pressure as you get closer to the green.

Ten holes on the Ocean Course run right next to the Atlantic, but the ocean is visible from every hole. Its presence can be felt on every hole as well, with ocean breezes pulling and pushing the ball all over the course. While it was nice of Dye to keep the rough to a minimum, the presence of expansive waste bunkers is no less difficult. The 207-yard par-3 fifth hole brings sand and water to the extreme, making the hole-length expanse of sand on the left the safest side on which to err. The par-5 seventh hole is reachable if the wind is at your back, but it is so tight near the green that any shot even slightly off line will likely yield a sandy third shot.

Perhaps Dye's greatest Ocean Course accomplishment came in 2002, when he was finally given permission to move the forty-yard deep eighteenth green closer to the ocean. He had long wanted to move the green to allow the elements to wreak even more havoc with approach shots. While we appreciate his desire to finish the course off in grander style,

would it be so hard to give players a break after seventeen grueling tests? Regardless of the end result, surviving the 439-yard monster in its new incarnation will make your challenging Ocean Course experience even more memorable.

Although the Ocean Course is the newcomer of publicly accessible Kiawah courses, any Kiawah fan will make a point—make that four points—to mention the great golf on the 10,000-acre barrier island. Cougar Point, Turtle Point, Osprey Point, and Oak Point represent a variety of styles carved in, around, and through the saltwater marshes and out onto the edges of the Atlantic. Jack Nicklaus's Turtle Point is an understated classic design that eases through hardwoods and palmettos. Three holes run along the ocean; a new antebellum-style clubhouse has just been added to the property, making it a great place to gather for a meal as well as a round of golf. Osprey Point is the most playable course on the island. Cougar Point is the shortest course, a build-out of an executive course, and features small green complexes that are a challenge.

The River Course (Tom Fazio, 1995) and Cassique (Tom Watson, 1999) are Kiawah's private clubs, open to property owners on the island.

Tall natural grasses wave in the ever-present winds at Kiawah, where another natural resource, sand, is used in waste bunkers that can run the entire length of holes.

The Ritz-Carlton Lodge, Reynolds Plantation
Greensboro, Georgia

The Ritz-Carlton Lodge,
Reynolds Plantation
One Lake Oconee Trail
Greensboro, GA 30642
Tel.: (706) 467-0600
Fax: (706) 467-0601
www.ritz-carlton.com

Designer: **Bob Cupp (Plantation Course); Jack Nicklaus (Great Waters Course); Tom Fazio (The National Course); Rees Jones (Oconee Course)**

Date opened: **1988 (Plantation); 1992 (Great Waters); 1997 (The National); 2001 (Oconee)**

Number of holes: **81**

Fees: **$85–$115**

Yardage/par: **6,698 yards, par-72 (Plantation); 7,048 yards, par-72 (Great Waters); 7,015 yards, par-72 (The National); 7,393 yards, par-72 (Oconee)**

Rating/slope: **71.7/128 (Plantation); 73.8/135 (Great Waters); 73.6/136 (The National); 75.5/143 (Oconee)**

Pro shop: **Offers the newest high-tech equipment and the best in high-end apparel**

Golf instruction: **For individual or group sessions, plus Dave Pelz Golf Scoring Game School**

Driving range/putting green: **Good range, large putting green**

Rentals: **Clubs**

The Ritz-Carlton never seems to need a road map. The company has a knack for finding just the right spot to build a hotel and spa and make it work. The chain's recent installation at Lake Oconee, Georgia, is a case in point. An hour from Atlanta, an hour from Augusta, and they've landed right in the wheelhouse of their target clientele. The Reynolds Plantation property, a big success of its own with the development of single-home communities on eight thousand acres and fifty miles of lakefront property, now has a partner and a built-in group of potential buyers.

The Ritz-Carlton Lodge, Reynolds Plantation pays homage to the Creek Indians, the first settlers on the lake. They also honor their guests' love of golf, giving them the chance to play eighty-one holes of championship courses designed by famed designers Jack Nicklaus, Rees Jones, Tom Fazio, and Bob Cupp.

GEORGIA's, Reynold's Plantation's signature restaurant, specializes in southern cuisine with gourmet flair. Regional ingredients such as pecans, peaches, and Vidalia onions boost the local flavor. The Linger Longer Bar and Grill specializes in dry aged beef, free-range poultry, and Maine lobsters in a laidback setting, and the Lobby Lounge gives you the chance to relax before or after dinner with a drink and Lake Oconee as your backdrop.

The 26,000-square-foot spa at The Ritz-Carlton Lodge holds the key to happiness for many guests. Whether you're looking to ease muscle soreness from a round of golf, or are in search of a full-fledged workout, the wellness center spa can get it done. The spa created a program based on the traditions of the Creek Indians, the first inhabitants of the Lake Oconee area. The Creek Indians' belief in the divination of the four seasons, the four corners of the compass, and the herbs, fruits, and flowers they bring has provided an abundant menu of spa experiences.

Of course, no matter how many holes of golf you play, no matter how many hours you spend in the spa, you can't leave Lake Oconee without spending some time on the water. Whatever your pleasure— swimming, fishing, boating, or water-skiing—it's available. And if you just feel like walking to the water's edge and sticking your pedicured toes in, that's fine too.

Lake Oconee's fingers and inlets allowed holes to be built that often lure golfers into places they'd rather avoid, but adventurous players might find it impossible to resist the chance to get just a bit closer for their approach shots.

THE GOOD NEWS: There are eighty-one holes of championship golf—designed by Rees Jones, Jack Nicklaus, Tom Fazio, and Bob Cupp—waiting for you to play at The Ritz-Carlton Lodge, Reynolds Planation. The bad news: You've only got a week. These courses provide a fair opportunity do some serious compare and contrast. If you find you just can't choose your favorite, why not stay? There could be a house available for you on the Reynolds Plantation residential property.

As for the courses, Rees Jones is the newest kid on the block with the three-year-old Oconee Course. The course is something of a departure for the man known as the "Open doctor" for his exceptional work with traditional designs. This risk/reward layout challenges golfers to choose between direct tee shots over inlets of Lake Oconee and long drives down tree-lined dogleg fairways. The course offers five holes in which Lake Oconee comes directly into play and four others tendering magnificent lake views.

Great Waters, the eighteen-hole Jack Nicklaus signature design, winds through densely wooded evergreen corridors only to open up to nine holes featuring the blue waters of Lake Oconee as the rough. Named one of the best courses in Georgia, second only to Augusta National, Great Waters proves to be one of the most aesthetically inspiring golf courses in the continental United States.

Bob Cupp, along with Hubert Green and Fuzzy Zoeller, used only the rolling Appalachian Mountain foothills as a blueprint for designing the Plantation Course. The course's wide fairways give the Plantation Course a more relaxing—and forgiving—layout for golfers of all abilities.

Tom Fazio's twenty-seven-hole masterpiece, The National Course, is a tight trip through towering pines, flowering dogwoods, and more than one hundred bunkers. For several holes Fazio used the shores of Lake Oconee and edges of the natural landscape to provide little margin for error as golfers try to make their way onto the large undulating greens.

Clockwise, from top left: The clubhouse provides a roost from which you can see most of the Reynolds property, while its proximity to the water allows boaters to use the slips to dock their crafts before their play a round; from sunrise to noontime to sunset, the colors that come off the water and through the scrub pines at Reynolds Plantation provide a natural glow all over the course.

The American Club
Kohler, Wisconsin

The American Club
444 Highland Drive
Kohler, WI 53044
Tel.: (800) 344-2838
Fax: (920) 457-0299
www.destinationkohler.com

Designer: **Pete Dye**

Date opened: **1988 (Blackwolf Run); 1998 (Whistling Straits)**

Number of holes: **72**

Fees: **$105–$270**

Yardage/par: **7,142 yards, par-72 (Blackwolf Run-Meadow Valleys); 6,991 yards, par-72 (Blackwolf Run-River Course); 7,343 yards, par-72 (Whistling Straits-Straits); 7,201 yards, par-72 (Whistling Straits-Irish)**

Rating/slope: **74.7/143 (Blackwolf Run-Meadow Valleys); 74.9/151 (Blackwolf Run-River); 76.7/151 (Whistling Straits-Straits); 75.6/146 (Whistling Straits-Irish)**

Pro shop: **High-end gear, including logoed PGA Championship merchandise**

Golf instruction: **Kohler Golf Academy offers general or specific one-day through four-day programs, utilizing Swing Solutions computer software**

Driving range/putting green: **Like everything else here, resources abound, and your game will benefit**

Rentals: **Clubs**

Most golfers know The American Club as "Kohler." It's the family name, a family business (albeit a big family business), and one of the last of the nation's true company towns. What is now the lodge began in 1919 as a rooming house for the plumbing giant's immigrant laborers and has grown into a fixture in the high-end golf-destination business.

The only Midwestern resort to earn AAA's five-diamond rating (which it has received for the last nineteen years), The American Club puts visitors on sensory overload. There is nothing on the grounds—whether it's the hotel, the restaurants, spas, or the majestic golf courses—that wasn't thought out in advance. The resort is on the National Register of Historic Places list and is the result of a master plan generated by the Frank Lloyd Wright Foundation. It was no surprise that Herb Kohler Jr. selected the "Mr. Wright" of golf-course design, Pete Dye (and his wife, Alice, and their son, P. B.), to be the guiding force behind the four courses. It is also fitting that Kohler found an antique solarium in Chorley, Lancashire, in northern England, bought it, had it dismantled, and then rebuilt it as the resort's Fountain Courtyard, where visitors can enjoy desserts, coffee, tea, and other goodies. River Wildlife and Inn on Woodlake offer more rustic lodging and activity options.

The Blackwolf Run courses, named after a Winnebago Indian chieftain, hosted the 1998 U.S. Women's Open. In 2004 the Whistling Straits complex will host the PGA Championship. As for the spa, do we really have to tell you just how well appointed that area is?

"AN HOUR NORTH OF MILWAUKEE" just doesn't have the same ring as " just south of the Caymans," does it? But don't let geographical parochialism get the best of you. The American Club provides pampering rivaled by precious few vacation destinations. A patriotic Americanism, begun by company founder Walter J. Kohler, is evidenced throughout the resort. Its 121 rooms are dedicated to prominent Americans (such as Abraham Lincoln and Teddy Roosevelt), but it also honors those who came to our shores, as evidenced by The Immigrant, a remarkable restaurant that links six rooms, each identified by an ethnic group that made the United States their new home. From trout to in-season game, the Continental restaurant is not to be missed. Neither is the Horse & Plow, a pub config-ured on the site of the club's former bowling alley. Its commitment to remain true to the resort's history is seen in the tables made of planks from the bowling alley. A variety of other casual dining and drinking spots are sprinkled throughout the resort, including fun and relaxing options at the courses' clubhouses.

Let's talk treatments. Actually, the remarkable amenities in the rooms (multihead showers, whirl-pools, steam enclosures) constitute spa treatments in and of themselves. But if you can tear yourself away from your own bathroom, head to the Kohler Waters Spa and try the Citrus Pine Sensation, where pine branches are rubbed on your body while warming and cooling waters are alternately run over you. The River Bath Inspiration allows you to sit in front of a roaring fireplace, getting a foot soak, scalp massage, and sugar scrub exfoliation. Then you get showered and prepared for a remoisturizing bath. While these two options sound hard to pass up, why not try the Sok Bath, in which you sit under cascading waters that produce champagne-like bubbles and pour into a pool brightened by colored underwater lights. A more forceful variation on the theme, the Tsunami, is a powerful water massage meant to stimulate the central nervous system, cleanse, and energize the skin. This is the best advertising the Kohl family could have, and it just so happens that there is a kitchen and bath showroom on the grounds.

Left: The grazing sheep won't laaaaaaaugh at an errant shot at the Irish Course and neither will you as you try to navigate around the tricky bunkers. Above: The Sheboygan River runs through the courses at The American Club.

TRYING TO DECIDE which course is best at The American Club is like asking someone if they prefer pizza with mushrooms or pepperoni. Both options are equally tasty, just a bit different from the other. The Pete Dye details make the choice ever harder: millions of cubic yards of moved dirt, dramatic twists and turns, dunes and tall grasses highlighting two miles of Lake Michigan shoreline intersected by ponds, creeks, and rivers. None of the courses have a slope rating lower than 140, but Dye did set up five sets of tees, so play from the appropriate spots to enjoy your round as much as possible.

At Whistling Straits, the Straits Course, which is walking only, was created out of an abandoned military site. The toxic storage areas were capped, the abandoned runways ripped up, and the storage sheds leveled. The fairways are forty yards wide; when the wind is up, you'll need every inch, but you'll enjoy the challenging shots as much as the equally taxing walk. "Pinched Nerve," the 223-yard seventeenth, features a twenty-foot bunker on the front left corner so aim for the right side of the green. "Dyeabolical," the 470-yard closing hole, is aptly named, featuring a sixty-four-yard green that makes just getting there an accomplishment.

The Irish Course approximates the Celtic experience, especially when that ever-present breeze freshens. The ninth hole, "Last Gasp," can be just that as you navigate forty-foot bunkers and watery go-no-go decisions from the tee. The 558-yard closing hole, "Black & Tan," will have you calling for one by the time you make it to the green.

At Blackwolf Run, Meadow Valleys and the River Course tease with holes such as "Gotcha," "Rise and Fall," "Gamble," and "Rolling Thunder." "Rise and Fall" is the River Course's eleventh, a 560-yard par-5 bending so far right that the green appears to be trying to work its way back to the tee. Of course, water hugs the right side all the way around. All in all, the courses are spectacular Dye, full of challenge, beauty, and a vision that makes you wish you could have looked through his eyes as he "saw" the finished product on his first visit.

Above: The Kohler fixtures make it difficult to leave the American Club's spa (left) or the mini-spas in the guest rooms (right). Right: The mist rises off Lake Michigan on the Straits Course.

The Ritz-Carlton, Lake Las Vegas
Henderson, Nevada

The Ritz-Carlton, Lake Las Vegas
1610 Lake Las Vegas Parkway
Henderson, NV 89011
Tel.: (800) 241-3333
or (702) 567-4700
Fax: (702) 567-4777
www.ritz-carlton.com

Designer: **Jack Nicklaus (Reflection Bay Golf Club); Tom Weiskopf (The Falls Golf Club)**

Date opened: **1998 (Reflection Bay); 2002 (The Falls)**

Number of holes: **36**

Fees: **$200–$220**

Yardage/par: **7,261 yards, par-72 (Reflection Bay); 7,250 yards, par-72 (The Falls)**

Rating/slope: **74.8/138 (Reflection Bay); 74.7/136 (The Falls)**

Pro shop: **32,000-square-foot clubhouse—if you can't find it, you don't need it**

Golf instruction: **For individual or group sessions, the Nicklaus/Flick offers some of the best instruction in the world**

Driving range/putting green: **Great views and pristine details make working on your game seem almost as much fun as playing a round**

Rentals: **Clubs and shoes**

We know that Las Vegas is the land of make-believe, a place where pirates battle in front of gawking tourists, replicas of Venetian canals and the Empire State Building spring from sidewalks, and millions of people believe they're going to leave with more money than they brought. But if the Lake Las Vegas Resort, just seventeen miles from the casinos and neon lights, had been in the area generations ago, Bugsy Siegel wouldn't have been so crazy and Frank Sinatra would never have moved to Palm Springs. The Ritz is the latest addition to this resort, which wraps hotels, shops, restaurants, townhouses, big houses, and exercise and spa facilities around part of the 320-acre man-made lake's shoreline.

Sailboats lollygag around the water, hills stretch for miles, and the village takes on the look of a Mediterranean town. Add the Ritz-Carlton vibe to this elegant outpost and you can feel completely removed from the Vegas glitz. The only time you get a glimpse of the hurly-burly is from the tenth tee or twelfth fairway of The Falls course, a dramatic 2002 Tom Weiskopf design that could necessitate motion-sickness medication for queasy players. The course that started it all, Reflection Bay, is Jack Nicklaus's first resort course in Nevada. This 1998 course runs five holes along the Lake Las Vegas shore and provides a stimulating challenge as well as lovely views of the property.

THE RITZ HAS 349 GUESTROOMS AND SUITES, all exhibiting the exemplary touches typical of this hotel. The 30,000-square-foot fitness center and Spa Vita di Lago provide the latest in cardiovascular and strength-training equipment, as well as twenty-four treatment rooms and an open-air meditation garden sunlit for yoga, stretching, and other movement classes. The spa is the only United States location for Italy's famed La Culla treatment and lies in its own warm elegant building with an exclusive entrance.

Guests who favor outdoor activities have the chance to choose from fly-fishing excursions for bass and trout, gondola rides on the lake, mountain biking, high-desert hiking, swimming, and beach sports.

Medici Café and Terrace, the resort's main restaurant, earned a spot in *Esquire* magazine's list of best new restaurants for 2003. You can sit indoors, but the al fresco option gives you the chance to imagine you're in a Tuscan villa with views of the lake, the gardens, and the desert sky. The weekend brunch offers access to a self-serve Bloody Mary bar; we recommend a post-brunch nap before you hit the casino. You can walk from the Ritz to the Hyatt's Casino Baraka, which is open only nineteen hours a day and gives players the chance to gaze out the two-story floor-to-ceiling windows. Casino MonteLago in the town center provides a mellow personalized approach to gaming. While all the standard games are available, the feel is more European destination than go-for-broke American fun.

Tom Weiskopf designed Lake Las Vegas's Falls Course, which was named for the two man-made waterfalls that cascade down the eleventh (left) and seventeenth (far left) holes. The course provides dramatic elevation changes and tricky forced carries over rocks and water.

JACK NICKLAUS BUILT REFLECTION BAY at Lake Las Vegas down at water level, with five holes playing right along the shoreline. The 199-yard eighth and 428-yard ninth holes are guarded on the left by the bright blue water. Pull a shot and you might as well just admire those sailboats skimming along the surface because your golf ball is history. Returning to the clubhouse, the 561-yard par-5 eighteenth bends right along with the water, but there are at least some mercifully placed bunkers along the edge of the greenery to keep some balls from rolling into the drink. Nicklaus has been fighting mightily for the last decade against innovations to the golf ball that he says make it travel too far. One development that he doesn't seem to mind is how the balls land softly and spin abruptly, keeping them from trickling off the sides of the elevated greens that dominate this course.

Tom Weiskopf got second pick of the land for The Falls, and while he admits that he wasn't thrilled about the property, he's created a layout that is dramatic and intimidating, and conjures up some of his spectacular Arizona courses. The course is named for the two man-made falls on the eleventh and seventeenth holes, but stumble on your Softspikes and you'll be taking a fall of your own down the three-hundred-foot rise at the tenth tee.

That amazing vista makes for a dramatic tee shot (and an exhilarating cart ride if you didn't check the brakes) and starts a backside that has drawn gasps and grunts from players trying to work their way around the uneven lies. The par-5 twelfth plays 553 yards from the tips, uniting the highest point on the course with a blind second shot through a narrow pass that ends with a two-tiered green perched on the side of a cliff and one of the best photo opportunities of downtown Las Vegas.

Nicklaus's other course, South Shore, is a private layout for property owners. Tom Fazio has just finished a course, Rainbow Canyon, which will open for play in 2004, and word on the street is that Greg Norman has been making exploratory visits to build what many say would be the resort's last course.

Right: Jack Nicklaus built the Reflection Bay course in the valley of the resort's property, allowing him to lay five holes right along the water.
Far right: The Mediterranean-style architecture makes Lake Las Vegas feel much farther away than its seventeen-mile drive from the Strip.

Four Seasons Resort Aviara
Carlsbad, California

Four Seasons Resort Aviara
7100 Four Seasons Point
Carlsbad, CA 92009
Tel.: (760) 603-6800
Fax: (760) 603-6801
www.fourseasons.com/aviara

Designer: **Arnold Palmer and Ed Seay**

Date opened: **1991**

Number of holes: **18**

Fees: **$175**

Yardage/par: **7,007 yards, par-72 to 5,007 yards, par-72**

Rating/slope: **74.2/137 to 69.1/119**

Pro shop: **High-end merchandise abounds; if you need it, they'll get it**

Golf instruction: **For group and individual sessions, at the Aviara Golf Academy by Kip Puterbaugh, one of the best in the world**

Driving range/putting green: **Expansive range and large putting greens, sand and chipping practice areas**

Rentals: **Clubs and pull carts**

San Diego County is an easy sell, at any time of the year. It is virtually always sunny, temperatures range from seventy to eighty-five degrees, the beach is a wedge away to the west, and dramatic hills loom to the east. Atop one of those hills, forty minutes north of downtown San Diego, the Four Seasons Resort Aviara provides views of the Batiquitos Lagoon, the waves of the Pacific Ocean crashing onto the beach, and the spectacular course built by Arnold Palmer and Ed Seay in 1991.

With typical Four Seasons flair, dining and unwinding is an unparalleled experience here. Golfers will be pampered in the 32,000-square-foot clubhouse by a staff that makes every visitor feel like a member of the swankest club in town. Whether you choose to use the pools, spa, fitness room, or deck chairs, pre-round, post-round, or in lieu of golf, the resort abounds with laid-back southern California cool.

There are plenty of places worth visiting off the resort grounds, from the charming town of Rancho Santa Fe to the kitschy Old Town section of San Diego and its bustling Gaslight District. Golf wonks find themselves in a little bit of heaven once they get off the course; Carlsbad boasts the greatest and most concentrated collection of golf-club design geniuses in the world. Callaway, TaylorMade, Titleist, and many other companies have headquarters in the neighborhood and you never know when you might overhear a lunch conversation among engineers, executives, or even some visiting tour players about what could become the next big thing in equipment.

THE TOWN OF CARLSBAD WAS NAMED for the famous spa in Karlsbad, Bohemia, which has similar minerals in its water. Translated as "village by the sea," you can feel the soothing effects of the ocean. Your blood pressure begins to drop the minute you park the car in front of the resort. As you saunter through check-in and sashay up to your room, you quickly get into the Four Seasons groove. Three of the resort's restaurants, California Bistro, the Ocean Pool Bar & Grill, and Argyle, offer alfresco dining and a perfect place to grab a cocktail for optimum sunset views. Vivage serves us contemporary Northern Italian cuisine in a sophisticated but casual setting.

Once you solve the golf-pool-spa or spa-golf-pool dilemma, you will find that the 15,000-square-foot spa and fitness area features indoor and outdoor treatment rooms, an indoor solarium, saunas, and steam rooms. You can get in-room or poolside massages or even take advantage of the couple's suite, which has side-by-side massage tables, a lounge, marble fireplace, shower for two, and private patio. The Watsu Massage gives you a chance to stretch and get a rubdown in a heated pool; you can even get an Avacado Body Wrap or a Nourishing Sugar Scrub to give yourself a spicy ginger scent and sweet glow.

If you're crazy enough to think about work while you're in this setting, the 331 rooms and suites are wired with high-speed internet access and other amenities necessary for communication with the home office (especially if you want to gloat to your coworkers). A post-treatment treat is a long walk around the many trails, which are perfect for checking out the native vegetation and bird-watching.

Opposite page: The scenery at Aviara is impressive; each hole features wild flowers, rocks, water, and various other impediments to par. This page: After the battering you'll likely endure on the course, the pampering begins— cozy rooms (top, left and right), pools (left), and spa treatments provide comfort for weary golfers.

THE GOLF COURSE at the Four Seasons Resort Aviara, carved expertly out of 180 acres, provides significant elevation changes from tees to greens, yielding some difficult uphill and downhill lies. The elevation changes provide great views of the lagoon, the ocean, and the mountains. A faint smell of rosemary comes from the lush vegetation. Daisies, hibiscus, and purple Batiquitos are planted in bursts along the edges of the holes; there's even a small but effective waterfall on the 146-yard par-3, guarded left and right by water. As you start making your way uphill, the par-5 fifth, a dogleg right, is a brutal three-shot hole full of sand cross bunkers and sandy greenside hazards. The sixth hole, a 195-yard par-3, plays about 215. Don't be short or you will be poking around in the aforementioned ornamental plantings.

The back nine turns up the pressure as the peaks and valleys get a bit steeper and the already large greens grow a bit more (all the better to three-putt as you try to negotiate the tricky reads). By the time you wind your way down to the eighteenth tee, a glorious view of the Spanish-style clubhouse, the lagoon, the ocean, and the 443-yard dogleg awaits you. The water running down the right side of the eighteenth hole tempts you into thinking you can bite off an extra 10 yards en route to a green sloped from back to front. The fairway is huge and the optimum corner-cutting drive needs to cover about 290 yards, so play it safe and take your chances on getting a long iron close enough for a closing birdie.

If you're in need of instruction, the Aviara Golf Academy is worth the time. A variety of sessions are available for players of all levels and the instruction staff will break down your swing, run you through a series of drills aimed at keeping your troubles from creeping back into your swing, and then reinforce how those drills can help you build a completely new—and dependable—swing.

Above: From the deck of the hotel pool, you can get a view of the Pacific Ocean and the Batiquitos Lagoon. Right: As you head down the hill to the seventeenth green, the Batiquitos glimmers in the sun.

The Inn at Spanish Bay
Pebble Beach, California

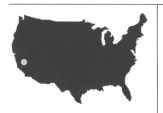

The Inn at Spanish Bay
2700 17-Mile Drive
Pebble Beach, CA 93953
Tel.: (800) 654-9300
Fax: (831) 622-3603
www.pebblebeach.com

Designer: **Charles Maud (Del Monte Golf Course); Robert Trent Jones Sr. (Spyglass Hill Golf Links); Robert Trent Jones Jr., Frank "Sandy" Tatum, and Tom Watson (The Links at Spanish Bay)**

Date opened: **1897 (Del Monte); 1966 (Spyglass Hill); 1987 (Spanish Bay)**

Number of holes: **54**

Fees: **$95–$250**

Yardage/par: **6,339 yards, par-72 (Del Monte); 6,862 yards, par-72 (Spyglass Hill); 6,821 yards, par-72 (Spanish Bay)**

Rating/slope: **71.6/125 (Del Monte); 75.3/148 (Spyglass Hill); 74.8/146 (Spanish Bay)**

Pro shop: **Shops at each course offer a variety of apparel (fair-weather and foul-weather gear), as well as equipment**

Golf instruction: **For individual or group sessions, through Golf Academy at Pebble Beach**

Driving range/putting green: **Available at all three courses**

Rentals: **Clubs and trolleys**

Although Pebble Beach Golf Links gets all the glory, the sister properties in the organization should not be overlooked. Of course, neither the Inn at Spanish Bay nor Casa Palmero ever voices an objection. They don't have to since there are enough proponents of these properties to keep them in business for years.

The 270-room Inn at Spanish Bay, just a couple of miles down 17-Mile Drive from Pebble Beach (whose course is also available to guests of the Inn at Spanish Bay; see pages 144–47), is the proud recipient of the Mobil Five-Star rating, too. Each room has its own fireplace, as well as a view of the ocean, the golf course, or the Del Monte forest. Casa Palmero, a Mediterranean-style estate visible to the right of Pebble Beach's first and second fairways, features twenty-four rooms and suites, some with whirlpool spa.

The three courses that make up the Inn at Spanish Bay are The Links at Spanish Bay, Spyglass Hill Golf Links, and Del Monte Golf Course. Charles Maud built Del Monte in 1897. The course, with its flattish design and small greens, still vexes players with their modern equipment and certainty that they should be able to tame it. Spyglass and Spanish Bay are a different issue altogether. They are broad-shouldered take-no-prisoner layouts that welcome wind gusts and inclement weather as just part of the show.

THE INN AT SPANISH BAY has four distinctly different dining options: Pèppoli, a casual Tuscan eatery where the wine flows and the food is fabulous; Roy's at Pebble Beach, an eclectic breakfast/lunch/dinner eatery featuring wood-fired pizzas; Sticks, a sports bar and casual restaurant specializing in comfort foods such as meatloaf, deli sandwiches, and chowder; and Traps, where there is a cozy fireplace lounge and bar. Appetizers, hors d'oeuvres, sports on television, and a broad single-malt selection are the selling points here. All four establishments provide great views of the property and the Pacific.

The Spanish Bay Club gives guests at the Inn a variety of state-of-the-art cardiovascular and weight-training equipment as well as professional instruction. A full indoor gym complements the outdoor swimming pool and Jacuzzi, massage studio, and other amenities aimed at revitalizing tired golfers. If you would rather do your roadwork on the road instead of on the treadmill, take the Spanish Bay Nature Walk through the Del Monte Forest. The scenery is spectacular as you walk through the sand dunes, coastal vegetation, riparian areas, and forest conservation area. Keep your eyes and ears open for a variety of sights and sounds from the wildlife on the beach and in the forest.

SPYGLASS HILL, designed by Robert Trent Jones the elder, provides a bit of Treasure Island with every hole. The names are right out of the book, and the course zigzags in and out of the forest. The first hole, a dogleg left par-5, starts out with a drive through the trees, but if you're lucky enough to cut the corner, you will find yourself facing the Pacific off in the distance while deer gallop all over the fairway and the sea lions shout from the beach. There is indeed treasure on every hole on this course.

The Links at Spanish Bay, designed by Robert Trent Jones Jr., Tom Watson, and Frank "Sandy" Tatum, is one of America's foremost Scottish-style linksland courses. The craggy Monterey coastline creates the lusty gusts of wind that blow incessantly along the layout. The course was built on what was once an old sand quarry. The 6,820-yard course is tough and authentic, conjuring up moments from "the auld grey toon." If the sand and wind don't get you, the tight shots will. The par-four fifteenth features a fairway landing area that is squeezed from the sides by iceplant and native grasses. Even the weather is cool, damp, and windy on most days. The course was also the first California course to earn membership into the Audubon Cooperative Society. From the rolling fairways to the white sand dunes to the melancholy strains of the bagpipe that signals the end of each day's play, the Links at Spanish Bay is a blustery challenging journey into the kind of golf that is difficult to find in the United States.

Del Monte Golf Course is the oldest continually operating course west of the Mississippi River. The folks there are proud to say the other contender for the title, the Presidio Golf Course, lost its crown when it was forced into temporary duty as a practice-drill field to prepare troops for the Spanish-American War. The 6,339-yard course has never had a major facelift and still hosts the California State Amateur and Pebble Beach Invitational tournaments. No water comes into play, but there are sixty-eight bunkers armed in the fight to protect par.

It doesn't get the attention of its sister course just a few miles away, but the Spanish Bay Golf Links is a dramatic, scenic, and windblown test of golf designed by Robert Trent Jones Jr., Tom Watson, and former United States Golf Association director Sandy Tatum.

Pebble Beach Golf Links
Pebble Beach, California

Pebble Beach Golf Links
1700 17-Mile Drive
Pebble Beach, CA 93953
Tel.: (800) 654-9300
Fax: (831) 625-8598
www.pebblebeach.com

Designer: **Jack Neville and Douglas Grant**

Date opened: **1919, with 1998 redesign of fifth hole by Jack Nicklaus**

Number of holes: **18, including a half-dozen of the most photographed holes in the world**

Fees: **$380**

Yardage/par: **6,737 yards, par-72**

Rating/slope: **73.8/142**

Pro shop: **High-end hard goods and apparel, as well as glassware and keepsake items**

Golf instruction: **For individual or group sessions**

Driving range/putting green: **Large putting green**

Rentals: **Clubs**

You've read about it, seen it on television from Bing to Bill Murray, and played it on your kids' video games, so it's no surprise that your first trip to Pebble Beach Golf Links conjures up full-blown emotional overload. As you try to remain calm, know this: there is nothing you will do—good or bad—that hasn't been done before. Know this too: they're expecting you and your frayed synapses. That's why guests can sign up for a twenty-five-minute pre-golf spa treatment that incorporates stretching and soft-tissue massage to align body and mind prior to tee time.

With your brain full of information and your camera full of film, your first round at Pebble, no matter how crowded the course may be, will go by faster than you can imagine. Policy for the Lodge (six spectacular rooms on the upper level and 161 rooms and suites spread among eleven buildings on the property) mandates two nights stay for every Pebble round you play, so stay at least four nights to get in two rounds. Lodge guests get preferred tee times at oceanside sister courses Spyglass Hill Golf Links and The Links at Spanish Bay, as well as the inland Del Monte Golf Course (see pages 140–43).

March through November are the busiest months and you can make reservations eighteen months in advance, so call ahead to get your perfect tee time: early morning access lets you play the course at its most pristine, while late afternoon rounds are perfect for Pacific sunset photo opportunities. Make the most of the experience by taking a caddie. They are professionals who will save you at least five strokes with impeccable reads on the greens and club selections that take into account ability, wind gusts, and nerves. They will also provide hilarious and interesting stories about the famous and not-so-famous devotees of what just might be the country's best golf course.

TO BORROW FROM THE GRADUATE, "Amenities, Benjamin. Amenities." Pebble Beach Golf Links spares no detail, from the fireplaces outside the garden suites, to Jacuzzis in the rooms, to restaurants that look out over first tee or the fabled eighteenth hole and its Pacific horizon. For the adventurous spa enthusiast, or drained hacker, there's even something called "Cranio-Sacral Therapy," a hands-on technique that results in deep relaxation for the brain and central nervous system. Another spa favorite is the post-golf treatment (in either fifty- or eighty-minute forms) that provides massage of the forearms, neck, lower back, and hips; it's geared as much toward preparing for tomorrow's round as it is toward recovering from today's. The Lymphatic Massage is a detoxification process that stimulates the immune system, shrinking that nasty cellulite and promoting weight loss.

Once you've experienced the resort's weight-control solution, you'll feel less guilty when you head for the restaurants. The Tap Room is a clubby steak-and-chops venue. Each dish has a hint of California flair, but don't hurry to your table; just grab a tumbler of Scotch and check out the out-of-this-world collection of golf memorabilia. The elegant Club XIX (jacket and tie required) offers a prix-fixe light French dining experience that makes ordering easy—there are two options each night. If you want to walk off that sumptuous meal, check out the Shops at Pebble Beach, which offer everything from art galleries and jewelry stores to an expansive shop full of golf items. While there is no reason to leave the compound, a side trip to Carmel-by-the-Sea, a slow ride down 17-Mile Drive, or a winery tour are worthwhile escapes.

THE COURSE AT PEBBLE BEACH GOLF LINKS that Jack Neville and Douglas Grant built in 1919 has been tweaked and cleaned up here and there, but the only real major addition came when the Pebble Beach Company bought back the lot along Stillwater Cove that was sold in 1915. Jack Nicklaus, who has called Pebble his favorite course in the world, was entrusted with creating the new par-3 fifth hole, and in 1998 he unveiled the 187-yard uphill hole perched forty feet above the beach.

The fifth hole is where the course truly begins its scenic glory, moving into the sixth hole, guarded closely on the right by shear cliffs that echo with the bellowing of sea lions sunning themselves as they dodge golf balls. The 103-yard seventh is the most

deceptive short hole in the United States. If the wind is at your back, the sand wedge might be too much club; if the wind is in your face, the five-iron might not be enough. The shot across the inlet from the fairway of the eighth hole to the green roughly eighty feet below makes you feel like you're hitting it off the face of the earth.

As you tackle the inland holes up and down the hills, dodging the thick kikuyu grass that borders the fairways, you can't help but start thinking about the final two holes. Standing on the tee of the 178-yard seventeenth hole, you think of Tom Watson's famous chip-in from the left fringe to clinch the 1982 U.S. Open, of just how far the Pacific continues behind the green, and of just how far the shot looks from the tee. Your best bet for making par is by staying on the front of the green that slopes hard from back to front.

On eighteen, once you've had someone take your picture on the narrow tee, you gape at the hole that is shaped like a "close parenthesis." You can't believe how much room there is on the right of the fairway and you err on the side of caution so you don't dunk a drive in the ocean. But if you can't carve a fairway wood around the towering tree that guards the green, you're in a tough spot as you try to make a par with the surf pounding and curious tourists watching to see if you played the hole better than they did.

Pebble Beach has one more method for making you treasure your round—it's one of a handful of U.S. courses that still allow players to wear metal spikes. They may be hard to find and you may have tossed out that old wrench, but if you've missed the sound of metal spikes on the pavement as you cross from one hole to the next, Pebble Beach can help you out. Is that considered part of the Cranio-Sacral Therapy?

The most famous golf course in the country got that way for a reason—Pebble Beach Golf Links is arguably the most picturesque of golf's greatest courses.

The Ritz-Carlton, Half Moon Bay
Half Moon Bay, California

The Ritz-Carlton, Half Moon Bay
One Miramontes Point Road
Half Moon Bay, CA 94019
Tel.: (650) 712-7000
Fax: (650) 712-7070
www.ritz-carlton.com

Designer: **Francis Duane and Arnold Palmer (Old Course);**
Arthur Hills (Ocean Course)

Date opened: **1973 (Old); 1997 (Ocean)**

Number of holes: **36**

Fees: **$125–$145**

Yardage/Par: **7,104 yards/par-72 (Old); 6,700 yards/par-72 (Ocean)**

Rating/slope: **75.0/135 (Old); 71.8/125 (Ocean)**

Pro shop: **Stocked with high-end merchandise, from equipment to apparel**

Golf instruction: **For group or individual sessions**

Driving range/putting green: **Solid practice area lets you work on your knockdown shots to cheat the wind before you have to try them on the course**

Rentals: **Clubs and shoes**

This lap-of-luxury destination is perched on a cliff overlooking the Pacific Ocean, making it difficult to find a more elegant and romantic setting. The folks at the Ritz, however, have outdone themselves here because in addition to giving hardcore golfers a taste of Scotland, they've found new ways to give spa enthusiasts (and ultimately, the windswept duffers in need of some breeze-free relaxation) a swanky coddling.

Although it is just forty-five minutes from downtown San Francisco, The Ritz-Carlton, Half Moon Bay is able to provide a sense of getting away from it all. Two-thirds of the rooms have ocean views; most have views of the Ocean Course and Old Course. In case you feel the need to leave the grounds, you can take a jaunt to the village of Half Moon Bay and check out the antiques shops, art galleries, and boutiques. At the water's edge, you can take classes in the yoga studio, go horseback riding on the beach, take a whale watching tour, or paddle a kayak.

If you're not interested in staying in the hotel, you can arrange a stay in one of the three guest cottages, all of which come with binoculars and telescopes to look for those giant sea mammals without leaving the comfort of the house. The 16,000-square-foot spa (the powers-that-be here inform us that the word is an acronym for *sanitas per aqua*, which translates to "health through water") faces the Pacific.

SPA ENTHUSIASTS on the lookout for a new treatment can pamper themselves at the Ritz-Carlton, Half Moon Bay with a Lavender Facial, which includes a mixture of organic herbs and floral essences native to the region. While the facial is being applied, you'll also be getting a face and neck massage. If this experience is too pedestrian, you can indulge in the special Pumpkin Body Peel; Half Moon claims to be the pumpkin capital of the world. The treatment is aimed at helping you shed a layer of dead skin cells, treat your dry skin, and get a boost of vitamin A. Once you finish the jack-o'-lantern act, you are then rubbed with a vitamin A-, C-, and E-laced body lotion.

If the fitness center is your thing, pick your favorite machines and stare out at the Pacific as you burn calories and mentally plan your next meal. In addition to the cardiovascular machines, there are weight machines, aerobic classes, and a "hot yoga" class, which essentially puts yoga enthusiasts together in a room roughly the temperature of Phoenix in August. Stretch, twist, rinse, and repeat. The men's and women's lounges include whirlpools, steam rooms, and saunas, but you might want to try the candlelit coed Roman mineral bath or oceanfront Jacuzzi as a perfect end to the perfect workout.

Prepare for a bit of Scottish golf at the Ritz-Carlton, Half Moon Bay, where the Old Course, designed by Arnold Palmer and Francis Duane, requires you to play along the humps and bumps—and away from the gorse.

MANY PLACES AROUND the United States claim to have "links-style" courses or conditions that make you swear you're in St. Andrews. Truth be told, they're lying. Half Moon Bay, however, is one of the spots that actually can get you close to channeling an Americanized vision of Old Tom Morris. This natural phenomenon (one part seaside cliff and requisite heavy breezes, two parts city-by-the-bay weather patterns, and voilà: mist, heavy mist, rain, and forty-mile-per-hour gusts!) is not something the resort shouts as a selling point. It's all low-key, but to golfers who tire of too-perfect conditions this is a little slice of heaven.

The Old Course, originally designed by Francis Duane and Arnold Palmer in 1973, is four years removed from a facelift by Arthur Hills. The course still has traditional Palmer elements—dogleg-lefts and big undulating greens—but the rolling terrain remains shielded primarily by the huge cypress trees and brush that line the holes. You've got sixteen holes to make your scores count, though, because you've got a tough fight ahead on seventeen and eighteen, which play along the ocean. The wind can wreak havoc on golfers after they've played virtually every hole wind-free. Make it through the 424-yard par-4 eighteenth without dumping any balls in the ocean and you've earned your single-malt scotch.

The Ocean Course, however, is another story. The protective vegetation from the Old Course is nowhere to be found on the course that Arthur Hills assembled in 1997. If the wind doesn't get the ball doing crazy things in the air, the humpy, bumpy fairways will, pushing and pulling shots over, around, and into deep bunkers and tall fescue grass. The prevailing wind is at your back on the outward nine holes, so launch your drives and make your birdies while you can, because once you turn back into the wind, it's going to take everything you've got to keep the ball out of the Pacific and advancing toward the hole. Remember, on the way back into the wind, widen the stance, shorten the swing, play the ball back, take an extra club, and keep the ball as close to the ground as you can.

The image of Half Moon looming in the distance is a welcome sight from the eighteenth tee, especially when the wind is howling and the rain is teeming and you're just trying to get in the house without dumping one more ball into the Pacific.

Princeville Resort
Kauai, Hawaii

Princeville Resort
5520 Ka Haku Road
P.O. Box 223069
Princeville, Kauai, HI 96722
Tel.: (800) 826-9644
Fax: (808) 826-1166
www.princeville.com

Designer: **Robert Trent Jones Jr.**

Date opened: **1989 (Prince Course); 1991 (Makai Course-Ocean Nine);**
1991 (Makai Course-Lakes Nine); 1993 (Makai Course-Woods Nine)

Number of holes: **45**

Fees: **$125–$175**

Yardage/par: **7,309 yards, par-72 (Prince); 6,886 yards, par-72 (Makai-**
Ocean/Lakes); 6,875 yards, par-72 (Makai-Ocean/Woods); 6,901
yards, par-72 (Makai-Woods/Lakes)

Rating/slope: **75.3/145 (Prince); 73.2/132 (Makai-Ocean/Lakes);**
72.9/131 (Makai-Ocean/Woods); 72.5/129 (Makai-Woods/Lakes)

Pro shop: **Princeville caters to the discerning traveler, so count on**
finding the highest-end apparel and equipment here

Golf instruction: **For individual or group sessions**

Driving range/putting green: **It's hard to find a more spectacular place to**
practice. From the range and the practice green, you can get views of
the Pacific, Hanalei Bay, and the lush terrain of the courses. The put-
ting green is a must to help you work out the tricky grain

Rentals: **Clubs and shoes**

As you make the drive along the hilly terrain to the Princeville Resort, you realize that you're atop Kauai's Pu'u Poa Ridge. But you don't realize just how high you've gone until you step into the resort's opulent lobby, look out through the back window, and get a bird's-eye view of the coast—you're on the ninth floor of what is the only resort in the state built into a bluff. You might be going down from there, but only in the elevator shaft because the resort is one of the most exquisitely appointed in the world. If, for some unfathomable reason, you get tired of the view, the golf, the swimming, and the other sundry outdoor pursuits, you can go to the resort's private movie theater. I can't imagine why you'd want to do that, but hey, it's your vacation.

The sheer magnitude of the place, its cool marble and pristine atmosphere, seems at odds with the tropical environs, but the friendly mellow spirit of Hawaii seeps out through the staffers. The twenty-three acres of Princeville possibilities provide dramatic views of Kauai's picturesque Hanalei Bay. You can choose from ocean kayaking, hiking, or spa visits or grab a longboard and head out to catch a wave or two.

The beachside pool is expansive and cool. There won't be a spontaneous game of beach volleyball breaking out here; people check in to chill out, pursue their passions, and reconnect with their loved ones. They're here to treat themselves, by themselves. As the salt air mingles with the local flowers, there is an intoxicating quality in every breath you draw.

THE PRINCEVILLE RESORT SHUTTLE will take you to the Prince Course and the Princeville Health Club and Spa, which has a large workout area, aerobics studio, and outdoor whirlpool, and a full menu of relaxing and rejuvenating treatments. The Limu Wrap (that's seaweed to you and me) is designed to shed dry skin, draw out excess water weight, and eliminate toxins.

The Café Hanalei is famous for its Friday evening seafood buffet and Sunday morning Champagne brunch. Local specialties and Pan-Asian influences are evident on the menus at the other dining establishments in the resort. The beachside restaurants are skilled at making exotic tropical drinks, the food is terrific, and the sun and breeze are equally delicious. Although the rooms and suites are luxuriously decorated and provide great views, why you wouldn't want to be outside in Hawaii is anyone's guess. The point is, once you leave the room in the morning, there's precious little reason to return until you need to clean up for dinner.

Princeville is less a Hawaiian-specific resort than an idealized tropical oasis. Whether you're on your honeymoon, second honeymoon, or just getting away to recharge your batteries, there is a sense that no request is impossible. An air of privacy allows guests to feel as though they're constantly being catered to. The perfect Princeville evening begins with sunset libations in the Living Room, the lobby bar with views of Hanalei Bay. You'll be inspired to share with your loved one all the daydreams you've ever had about chucking the corporate world and opening your own tiki bar/bowling alley. Of course, the fact that you can even enjoy a private dinner, complete with personal service in your room or at your secluded beach or poolside dining spot, should also make you realize that tiki bar owners rarely enjoy these kinds of perks.

THE PRINCE COURSE, named after Prince Albert, the only son of King Kamehameha IV and Queen Emma before the island was colonized, gets all the publicity befitting royalty. Built in 1991 by part-time Hawaii resident Robert Trent Jones Jr., the course is a tough test, but in typical Jones fashion, it is a challenge that is harder from fairway to green than from tee to fairway. Long ranked the top course on the island, it offers spectacular views of the Pacific and the lush rain forest. The seventh hole, a 205-yard par-3, runs parallel to the ocean, providing amazing views of Anini Beach and the opportunity to test yourself against a wind that is always in your face. The 418-yard thirteenth hole, where a stream about 240 yards off the tee splits the fairway, cuts through the jungle; the green is situated against a waterfall backdrop. Hit the ball sideways on this course, and you'll need a machete to dig it out of the tropical growth.

The Prince gets all the attention, but the twenty-seven-hole Makai is just as regal in its playability and beauty. The locals say that *makai* means "closest to the ocean," and the aptly named Ocean Nine of the Makai Course provides even more dramatic panoramas than the Prince boasts. The Lakes and Woods nines layouts each offer plenty of what the names indicate, all of which makes for courses that can be played three different ways on three different days, with a player being hard-pressed to say which one is better.

Clockwise, from top right: The hotel at the Princeville Resort seemingly finds a way to get every guest a view of the ocean, and the pool provides another optical illusion, making you feel as though you could swim right off the edge; the golf courses give you perfect vistas from which to see balls soaring into lush green fairways.

One&Only Palmilla
San Jose del Cabo, Mexico

One&Only Palmilla
Km 7.5 Carretera
Transpeninsular
San Jose Del Cabo
BCS, CP 23400 Mexico
Tel.: (800) 637-2226
Fax: 011-52-624-146-7001
www.oneandonlyresorts.com

Designer: **Jack Nicklaus**

Date opened: **1996**

Number of holes: **27 (Mountain, Arroyo, and Ocean nines)**

Fees: **$105–$185**

Yardage/par: **3,602 yards/par-36 (Mountain); 3,337 yards/par-36 (Arroyo); 3,548 yards/par-36 (Ocean)**

Rating/slope: **74.3/144 (Mountain-Arroyo); 74.4/146 (Mountain-Ocean); 74.8/145 (Ocean-Arroyo)**

Pro shop: **Golf shop located at the course with an array of merchandise from logo practice balls to golf shirts and equipment**

Golf instruction: **Individual sessions, available by appointment**

Driving range/putting green: **Practice range is the best place to get comfortable while acting nonchalant about the scenery around you**

Rentals: **Clubs**

PGA Tour players are among the world's most avid sportsmen, and nothing gets between them and great fishing. So many years ago, legends such as Jack Nicklaus and Tom Weiskopf would come to the southern tip of Cabo San Lucas, known as Land's End, where the Sea of Cortez meets the Pacific Ocean. Traveling down Highway 1 from the airport, the twenty-five-mile drive features beach on the east side of the road and dramatic mountains and desert on the west. While Nicklaus was waiting for the sportfish to bite, he got to thinking about landing something else—a chance to build a golf course on a piece of land that would yield some of the most dramatic and beautiful holes in the world.

Nicklaus grabbed a spot north of Cabo, in the hills above the opulent One&Only Palmilla resort. It might take a lot of moxie to call yourself "One&Only," but the resort is matched in details and inspiration only by Nicklaus's twenty-seven-hole course—the Mountain, Arroyo, and Ocean nines. The intimate resort itself was founded in 1956 by Don Abelardo Rodriguez, son of General Abelardo Rodriguez, the interim president of Mexico, and has been a favorite retreat for the Hollywood set and other modern adventurous souls who make the quick trip from Los Angeles. An $80-million renovation of the resort has made this desert oasis even more appealing.

THE 115-ROOM HOTEL at the One&Only Palmilla is a mixture of extreme color, from the remarkable shades of blue that match the Sea of Cortez, where gray whales migrate in March, to the vibrant green strips of the golf course rising through the desert and falling like a verdant cascade to the coastal holes. Whitewashed walls, terra-cotta roofs, and tiled fountains create a natural soothing haven.

The hotel is perched on the hillside and the rooms all provide views of the sea. Telescopes for stargazing and whale-watching are available in each room. As you feel the thick cool ceramic tiles beneath your feet and turn on the flat-screen satellite television with DVD/CD player and Bose system surround sound, you realize just how hard it will be to leave the room for the outdoor world.

Every massage at the resort's spa begins with a ritual foot wash, a symbolic cleansing to rid stress.

After your massage, the lush villa garden allows you to order a refreshment and take a rock shower. Relax even more in the shiatsu whirlpool or stretch in the yoga garden. From snorkeling and scuba-diving to fishing or boating, there are any number of ways to spend the day outside in this place that sees roughly ten rainy days each year. A drive a few miles north into San Jose or twenty miles south into Cabo San Lucas provides interesting shopping and the chance to take advantage of an extremely favorable exchange rate.

Clockwise, from above: Jack Nicklaus's Ocean Nine winds down from the mountaintop to the sea; his Arroyo Nine snakes through canyons and valleys; the free-form pool at the resort; all rooms at Palmilla offer a patio or balcony with views of the sea.

VIRTUALLY EVERY WAVE, every cactus, and every arroyo is visible from the One&Only Palmilla's clubhouse on the top of the hill. From here, you can choose your course, mixing and matching the Mountain, Arroyo, and Ocean nines. Regardless of which course you choose, they all play from roughly 6,900 yards. The courses offer five sets of tees, which make the yawning chasms that stretch from one green patch to the next only slightly more terrifying than if you're playing from the appropriate tees. The elevation shifts dramatically and, in some cases, quickly enough to make you wish you had a burro instead of a golf cart.

The Mountain Nine starts by going directly away from the clubhouse but cuts back around and intersects with the Arroyo (that's Spanish for "there goes another brand-new Titleist") Nine. Water hazards come into play on a few of the holes on the original Palmilla eighteen but this is a Nicklaus design—don't miss the greens or you'll be facing tough bunker shots. The Ocean is a mix of long straightforward par-4s; you'll succeed on the par-3s and par-5s if you have a hint of Jack's trademark accurate long game. Making your way down the third hole is like taking a walk to the beach, culminating with a couple of putts on a green that might just as well be considered beach. The surf and sand don't come into play, but your imagination will as you gaze out to sea.

Although the bird's-eye view (right) shows just how much private beach is available to Palmilla guests, the resort's pools (above) are an inviting option as well.

The Ritz-Carlton Golf & Spa Resort, Rose Hall
Rose Hall, Jamaica

The Ritz-Carlton Golf & Spa Resort, Rose Hall
One Ritz-Carlton Drive
Rose Hall, St. James, Jamaica
West Indies
Tel.: (876) 953-2800
Fax: (876) 953-2501
www.ritz-carlton.com

Designer: **Robert von Hagge and Rick Baril**

Date opened: **2000**

Number of holes: **18**

Fees: **$125–$225; $85 for twilight rounds**

Yardage/par: **6,719 yards/par-71**

Rating/slope: **74.0/139**

Pro shop: **Well-appointed high-end equipment and apparel**

Golf instruction: **For individual or group sessions**

Driving range/putting green: **Wide practice range has plenty of practice targets, ocean views to the left, mountain views to the right; practice green in front of the clubhouse almost as slick as greens on the course**

Rentals: **Clubs and shoes**

Annee Palmer, the evil nineteenth-century temptress/owner of the 4,000-acre Rose Hall sugarcane plantation, may have been known as the White Witch, but she apparently didn't see fit to place a curse over this remarkable West Indies haven. Even the shuttle bus from the airport seems to have therapeutic powers as you daydream of fresh fish, cold Red Stripe beer, and birdies on the spellbinding course that bears Ms. Palmer's nickname. The resort spares no luxury appointments and displays the trademark soothing colors, mahogany detailing, and authentic Jamaican touches that make you feel completely, and contentedly, away from home. Just listen to the lilting patois of those poised to keep you happy and you'll be parroting the "no problem, mon" mantra of the locals, even as you tackle the treacherous and dramatic course carved out of six hundred tropical hillside acres. Panoramic views of the Caribbean can be seen on sixteen of the course's eighteen holes.

But remember, no matter how difficult the game becomes, the resort waits below. As you stare at the blue water that laps laconically against your ankles and contemplate round two with the White Witch, you might want to consider a Rose Hall sports massage to continue the supernatural experience.

TO BORROW A PHRASE FROM Jamaican reggae legend Bob Marley, there is a "positive vibration" in every nook and cranny of the Ritz-Carlton Resort at Rose Hall. The rooms are decorated in soothing tones and elegant details, the small balconies are perfect for early-morning or late-evening ocean gazing. There are plenty of activities available—from sailing to snorkeling to jet skiing (at the nearby beach club) to simply lounging—depending on your motivation level. The fully equipped fitness center gives you access to a variety of weight-training and cardiovascular machines, while the tennis court is the perfect place to work on your backhand in the brilliant sunshine. Afterward, the saunas, steam rooms, and relaxation lounges await. If you're here to be pampered, you won't lack for options. The 8,000-square-foot spa provides open-air or enclosed spaces, in which you can be poked, prodded, wrapped, or rubbed. From the rose body wrap or the cornmeal body scrub to the four-hands massage (where two people work in synchronicity around your body), you'll feel the tension melt away.

Dining and drinking options at Rose Hall come in many moods. The formal and elegant Jasmine's restaurant offers the self-proclaimed "jamasian" fusion of Jamaican and Asian flavors. Horizons offers romantic and secluded terrace settings for continental tastes, and Mango's is a traditional casual American and Caribbean poolside restaurant. For some early fun, check out the Reggae Jerk Center, open from noon to six o'clock in the evening. It offers native "jerk" recipes right on the beach and reggae bands set the mood.

SETTLE INTO ROSE HALL'S DRIVING RANGE to loosen up for your round at the White Witch Course and you'll be greeted by your "golf concierge" ("forecad-

die" to you and me), who gives you a brief overview of the course, which opened in August 2000. Once you feel comfortable, head to the first hole, a spectacular downhill par-4 that feels as though it's cascading down to the Caribbean.

As you wind your way up, down, and through the lush hillside, remember that like most Robert von Hagge designs, it's not as terrifying as it initially looks. Be patient, pick the risk/reward option you feel most comfortable with, and you will be able to navigate your way around the course with minimum difficulty. The course features dramatic elevation changes, especially on the par-5s and par-3s; the approach shot on the par-3 twelfth drops one hundred feet. To the left of that tee, you will see the home of the late Johnny Cash, where he lived for the last twenty-five years of his life.

Also, beware: Annee Palmer, the aforementioned White Witch, always seems to inspire some quirky bounces, some good and some bad. Balls have curiously rocketed at ninety-degree angles into bunkers and putts have rolled two feet uphill past the hole only to quiver and roll directly back into the cup, so don't take your eye off the ball for a second.

Clockwise, from bottom far left: Rose Hall's White Witch cuts a crazy swath through the Jamaican landscape; designer Robert von Hagge created a layout that is breathtaking but can be managed without giving up too many shots to par; back at the resort, the thatched-hut dining room provides access to gently blowing breezes and the lilting rhythms of the reggae bands that play on the sand; a room at the hotel.

Westin Rio Mar Beach Resort & Golf Club
Rio Grande, Puerto Rico

Westin Rio Mar Beach Resort & Golf Club
6000 Rio Mar Boulevard
Rio Grande, PR 00745-6100
Tel.: (888) 627-8556
Fax: (787) 888-6600
www.westinriomar.com

Designer: **Tom and George Fazio (Ocean Course); Greg Norman (River Course)**

Date opened: **1972 (Ocean); 1923 (River)**

Number of holes: **36**

Fees: **$85–$190, depending on season**

Yardage/par: **6,782 yards, par-72 (Ocean); 6,945 yards, par-72 (River)**

Rating/slope: **73.8/132 (Ocean); 74.5/135 (River)**

Pro shop: **Fully stocked with logoed wear, equipment, and casual tropical wear**

Golf instruction: **Instruction available for individuals or groups**

Driving range/putting green: **Good range, large putting green**

Rentals: **Clubs**

Five hundred acres, a mile of beach, and six hundred rooms and suites give this staple of Puerto Rican golf and hospitality a resonance with generations of guests. With average daytime temperatures of about eighty-one degrees and water temperatures that mirror that of the air, this island one thousand miles south of Miami has all of the perks of Florida's climate, without all of the humidity.

To be sure, the resort also makes full use of its proximity to Old San Juan, the El Yunque rain forest, and other destinations perfect for active visitors. While there will always be people on the lookout for shopping opportunities, the property offers plenty of recreational options sure to hold your interest for the duration of your stay. Free-form pools, a waterslide, water sports, a spa and fitness center, and a couple of great golf courses provide enough incentive to never get in a rental car or on a shuttle bus. The venerable Ocean Course has always lured people to the island, but the newer River Course, designed by Greg Norman, continues to get great reviews.

ALTHOUGH WESTIN RIO MAR provides everything you'll need for a great stay right on its grounds, there are also a variety of options for those who wish to explore the island of Puerto Rico. If you want to see Old San Juan, a shuttle will drop you off and give you the chance to shop and wander around the sixteenth-century San Cristobal Fortress, gothic cathedrals, and art galleries. Visit the El Yunque tropical rain forest, the only one in the U.S. National Forest System, which covers twenty-eight-thousand acres and rises to 3,624 feet. You will be witness to more than 240 different species of trees and more than two hundred species of birds. Take nature walks and fitness hikes or follow twenty-three miles of trails through rushing waterfalls to view clusters of tiny orchids and other exotic flowers amid the lush greenery. You can also go on a guided tour of the Camuy Caves and marvel at underground crystalline-stone formations, stalactites, stalagmites, and underground rivers and lagoons, or travel through the Camuy Valley past picturesque haystack hills, small villages, and large plantations. The Hacienda Carabali Horseback Ride gives you the chance to follow a trail guide down the mountainside and across streams to the bordering lowlands of Rio Mar.

If you're feeling lucky, you might want to try your hand in the casino, where you can choose from blackjack, poker, slot machines, and other games of chance. Beach lovers can choose from volleyball, windsurfing, waverunners, parasailing, fitness walks, or even merengue lessons on the sand. Whether you've always been a diver or have just watched *Finding Nemo* one too many times, a variety of scuba dives or snorkeling excursions will give you a glimpse of the vibrant underwater life. With water temperatures that hover around eighty degrees, and with about sixty feet of visibility, the dives that go thirty to seventy feet provide a weightless way to enjoy the coral reefs. A little nurturing in the spa can include anything from a firming seaweed wrap to an antistress full body treatment.

Left and above: The steady but warm tropical breezes are still blowing through the Ocean Course that George Fazio and his nephew Tom built more than 30 years ago.

IT'S HARD TO BELIEVE THAT the Ocean Course at Westin Rio Mar was built thirty years ago by George Fazio; it was also the first time his nephew Tom was credited for his contributions to the design. While the first and tenth tees here are so close to the clubhouse and al fresco bar ("Home of the World's Coldest Beer") that you can't ignore the hecklers as they kill time before they tee off, the proximity of the world's coldest beer will no doubt help take your mind off your ill-fated beginning.

Dogleg-lefts abound on the course, so if you aren't a lefty you might want to work on your draw while you're on the practice tee. That said, even if the wind happens to push your shots to the right, the fairways are generous enough to keep you safe. The greens, however, are large and overly mounded, making it tough for the greenkeepers to find spots to stick the pins so that players have even a remote shot at getting the ball close to the hole.

Greg Norman's River Course is framed by vistas of mountains and the Caribbean. His preservation of native foliage and use of preserved wetlands as obstacles create a natural feel for the course. The terrain seems to have remained intact, not subject to the whims of an architect who had a preconceived notion of what the course would look like before he even got to the property. Ideal for players of all skill levels, the design features wide fairways, open greens, shallow bunkers, and light rough, giving golfers of all abilities the chance to hit approaches into greens that, for the most part, are large and accessible. Over the years, Norman has become increasingly adept at building green complexes that accept low running shots from high-handicappers, while also being supple enough to handle high spinning shots from skilled players. He has developed a way to reward good shots and penalize poor shots without costing the player two strokes. Of course, the River Course does meander around the Mameyes River and assorted tropical wetlands, so if you hit a bad enough shot, you're going to have to reload. For that misstep, no course architect should be blamed.

Above and right: Greg Norman took a lush piece of tropical property and built the River Course, a risk-reward complement to the Westin Rio Mar's original course, the Ocean Course.

Off the Beaten Path

Many of the resorts in this section are old favorites that enjoyed local fame for decades but were eventually "discovered" by some city slicker who told a friend, who told another, and another. Now they are golf's version of an overnight success. You may need a connecting flight or have to spend some time in a rental car, but these resorts are incredible options—and many times tremendous bargains—that will provide spectacular scenery and a true sense that you've escaped your all-too-familiar world.

176   182   188   194   200

Grand View Lodge
Nisswa, Minnesota

Grand View Lodge
23521 Nokomis
Nisswa, MN 56468
Tel.: (800) 432-3788
Fax: (218) 963-2269
www.grandviewlodge.com

Designer: **Joel Goldstrand (The Pines), Mike Morley (The Preserve), Arnold Palmer/Ed Seay (Deacon's Lodge)**

Date opened: **1990 (The Pines); 1996 (The Preserve); 1999 (Deacon's Lodge)**

Number of holes: **63**

Fees: **$48–$88 (The Pines and The Preserve); $55–$98 (Deacon's Lodge)**

Yardage/par: **6,837 yards, par-72 (Pines-Lakes/Woods); 6,874 yards, par 72 (Pines-Woods/Marsh); 6,883 yards, par-72 (Pines-Marsh/Lakes); 6,601 yards, par-72 (The Preserve); 6,964 yards, par-72 (Deacon's Lodge)**

Rating/slope: **74.1/143 (Pines-Lakes/Woods); 74.3/145 (Pines-Woods/Marsh); 74.2/145 (Pines-Marsh/Lakes); 71.9/131 (The Preserve); 73.8/128 (Deacon's Lodge)**

Pro shop: **Fully stocked shops at all locations**

Golf instruction: **For individual or group sessions**

Driving range/putting green: **Good range and putting green**

Rentals: **Clubs and pull carts**

Quick, name the state in the nation with the most golfers per capita. Stop thinking, it is Minnesota. Before you make any jokes, the golf season here extends from April to late October or early November. Maybe they're a bit more impervious to chill factors than the rest of us and can extend their season, but this state is also a favorite with the United States Golf Association and Professional Golf Association of America, hosting a number of major championships. While the advent of Minnesota as a golf destination might be relatively new (especially if you weren't paying attention), it has yielded a boom in affordable and challenging golf courses that are taking up some of the land not covered by those ten thousand lakes. The state has Grand View Lodge to thank for its evolution.

A staple in laid-back family entertainment, Grand View is a rustic throwback. Opened in 1919, it has seen generations of visitors come for pure air, relaxation, and the kind of irony-free enjoyment that comes from canoes, fishing, walking in the woods, and other simple outdoor pleasures. Once the Grand View's management saw how people around the state had golf clubs in their trunks along with the poles and waders, they knew that it was time to add big-league golf to its complex. So the resort that built an enclosed lakeside pool that can fit three-hundred people in inclement weather and added the Glacial Waters Spa commissioned the construction of a golf course that turned into twenty-seven holes. Then they bought a course down the road, and got a guy named Arnold Palmer to build another one.

THE LODGE AT GRAND VIEW, which features exposed beams, rustic appointments, a number of dining options, and a strict commitment to down-home hospitality and understated fellowship, has continued to expand the operation where it can. In addition to the twelve rooms in the lodge, there are sixty-five cottages (ranging in size from one to eight bedrooms), as well as nine cabins at Gull Haven, the ten Roy Lodge cabins tucked into a stand of Norway pines, and the three- and four-bedroom townhouses/clubhouse suites built along the Pine Course's eighth fairway.

In addition to horseback-riding trails, water-ski boats, jet skis, other activities include sailing, canoeing, and biking. Of course, just admiring the trees rimming the lake from a beach chair isn't bad either. Between the beach and the lodge is the indoor activity center, with a second-floor fitness center and huge first-floor pool that has full-size basketball hoops and backboards attached to the side of the pool for a game of acquaball. Kids will never leave the 110-foot spiraling water slide that is the centerpiece of this 8,820-square-foot complex, which also features connecting pools, hot tubs, fountains, and industrial-strength water guns.

The Glacial Waters Spa, an Aveda Concept Resort facility, offers some decidedly funky treatments, including a Rosemary Mint Awakening Wrap, and the Purifying Stone Massage, which uses sage, cedar, and sweetgrass. But perhaps the most surprising treatment is the Himalayan Rejuvenation Treatment. Based on Ayurveda, the ancient healing art of India, it incorporates exfoliation and massage with a continuous warm stream of water applied to the forehead (apparently to calm the mind and relieve tension).

Top and bottom: The twenty-seven holes of the Pines Course, right across the street from the Grand View Lodge, feature nines that are cut through and around marsh, lakes, and woods. Play the three in various combinations and you'll get a good cross-section of the Minnesota golf experience.

THE TWENTY-SEVEN HOLES at The Pines, directly across the street from the Grand View Lodge, are comprised of the Lakes, Woods, and Marsh nines. Built in 1990, the permutations available create courses just north of 6,800 yards. The courses feature long carries, tricky greens, and storybook scenery.

The Preserve features dramatic elevation changes, including thirteen elevated tees. The 438-yard fifth hole requires a 250-yard drive over wetlands. Once you see the ball clear the marsh, you have until you reach your ball to calm down, and then you'll have about 180 yards of carry to the green for your next shot.

The Deacon's Lodge vibe is just pure golf. The huge driving range and putting greens are perfect for practice junkies. The on-site golfers create a low-key sensibility. As if to further prove that you can be an award-winning destination and still embrace the simple things, the resort offers a trolley that you can rent for five dollars in which you can pull clubs around the course, rather than riding the typical electric golf cart.

Put Deacon's Lodge east of the Mississippi and you'd be paying about $200 for the privilege to stick the tee into the ground. Of course, put it anywhere besides Minnesota and you lose the lakes, the cleaner-than-Ivory-Snow air, and the mixture of mature birch and pine trees. Birch trees are everywhere here, and if you're lucky enough to play one of the courses where the birches are right next to the shore and the streams are running fast, you'll see the tannic acid that seeps into the water, making it look like a lager roaring through. Many of the traditional Palmer designs are evident—wide fairways, dogleg lefts, and plenty of tricky risk/reward options. Pay particular attention on the 432-yard seventh hole, a rare dogleg-right, which features a double green. Check pin placement before you tee it up or you'll be faced with what you thought was a perfect drive only to realize that you'll have a huge second shot to get back in birdie range. The seventeenth hole, a two-hundred-yard par-3, features marsh on three sides and a lake that seems to stretch into Canada. To put a cap on the day, down a couple of cold beers and eat a walleye sandwich (the state staple, which each eatery claims it prepares without equal).

The rustic accommodations at Grand View Lodge are comfortable and the fireplace is a welcome weapon to ward off the chill (top), but the huge indoor water park/workout facility (bottom, left) and the lakeside cabins (bottom, right) are a hit with children and adults alike.

Coeur d'Alene Resort
Coeur d'Alene, Idaho

Coeur d'Alene Resort
115 South 2nd Street
Coeur d'Alene, ID 83814
Tel.: (800) 688-5253
Fax: (208) 664-7276
www.cdaresort.com

Designer: **Scott Miller**

Date opened: **1986**

Number of holes: **18**

Fees: **$160–$180**

Yardage/par: **6,804 yards, par-72**

Rating/slope: **69.6/121**

Pro shop: **Full of apparel, equipment, and gear to beat the chill**

Golf instruction: **For individual or group sessions**

Driving range/putting green: **Range faces the lake, making practice the most scenic you may have ever enjoyed**

Rentals: **Clubs and shoes**

Sure, you've heard of target golf, but Coeur d'Alene offers moving-target golf. This resort, built in 1986, is famous for its fourteenth hole, the 158-yard par-3 that features an island green in the middle of the lake for which the resort is named. The green is moved around the lake every day, changing the experience for golfers who will likely play the course many times during their stay.

While you might be tempted to think of this place as a one-trick pony, don't be fooled. The Coeur d'Alene Resort, on the northern tip of the Idaho panhandle, is a treat precisely because no one affiliated with it wants golfers to see the hole, conquer (or butcher) the hole, and get on the next plane back home. Just miles from Spokane, Washington, this location is one of the most pristine spots in the nation. The town's name, given to it by French traders, is loosely translated as "sharp-hearted." From one of the 337 rooms and suites in the eighteen-story tower, you'll see colors you never knew existed in nature and at 2,152 feet above sea level you'll breathe air clearer than ever before. Bring your fishing gear, your hiking shoes, and your binoculars because after tackling the course—which does have seventeen other scenic and challenging parkland holes—you will want to soak up the pristine natural beauty you can no longer find at home. Once you are hooked on the golf, you might wind up returning for the ski season.

THE COEUR D'ALENE HAS A FLEET of six boats, which can handle ten to four hundred people. The cruises can be lunch, dinner, or cocktail excursions, generally running about ninety minutes. In addition, you will also navigate through the St. Joe River, which is the highest navigable river in the United States. There are sunset cruises and brunch cruises, but make sure you look up often from the buffet line because you will have a good chance of seeing a bald eagle spear a Kokanee salmon out of the water while deer and other wildlife act unimpressed along the shore.

The resort boasts five restaurants available for dining. Beverly's is the signature restaurant, and features salmon, Idaho red ruby trout, and other Northwest specialties prepared in a display kitchen. The views of the lake, Boardwalk Marina, and surrounding mountains are spectacular, but if you don't want to just gawk through the windows, the Beachouse is your best bet. Right on the water at Silver Beach, next to the golf course, the views at this restaurant are spectacular and the food (whether it's seafood, steaks, or barbecued chicken in an Idaho huckleberry sauce) is tasty. The heated outdoor deck allows you to breath in the fresh air, which enhances the food.

If you want to get your exercise done inside, there are plenty of options in the fitness center. The folks at the Euro Spa make no bones about the fact that they want you for at least ten days; they've got a special program based on ten to twenty-one days of treatment. From thermal mineral water to algae, mud, oils, and herbs, you will be rubbed, anointed, basted, and scrubbed until you have absolutely no desire to return to the grind that is your everyday life.

The up-and-back layout of the course at the Coeur d'Alene gives players a chance to get more views of the lake, while the wide fairways allow golfers to be more aggressive off the tee and be a little more cautious on their approaches into the green.

THE LOVINGLY RESTORED wooden boats pull up to the marina to ferry you over to the course (it's a common theme—you take a boat out to the fourteenth green, too). Once there, you can warm up by hitting balls into the water; don't worry, they're sucked back to a shore-side way station to be used again and again. The resort is thrilled to be unveiling its new renovation of Miller's design; the course was beefed up with an additional five hundred yards, new tees were added, and fairway bunkers were restored. More than 250 trees were planted; this should go a long way toward tightening the course, which was previously exceedingly forgiving of stray tee shots.

The fifth hole has been redesigned, and will play at 158 yards, but a bunker that looks like a spreading paramecium threatens your equilibrium from the tee. The 313-yard par-4 thirteenth is a tricky hole along the shoreline, featuring a finger of water that sticks into the middle of the fairway about one hundred yards from the green.

Of course, the fourteenth is the hole that first brought attention to this course, and it is indeed worth taking numerous whacks at it (ideally, not during just one round). The green is twenty-four yards deep and thirty-two yards wide. In the setting, smack in the middle of the lake in front of the mountains, it feels about three feet square. Just take a deep breath, make sure you have the right club, and trust yourself. If you wind up in the drink, tell your playing partners that you hit it right where the green was the day before.

The movable island green at the fourteenth hole (above, right) was the impetus for all the buzz about the Coeur d'Alene, but recent renovations to the course have made it even more inviting. The hotel provides views of the lake and hills, and the expansive marina (right) is home to a variety of seafaring vehicles for guests.

Bandon Dunes Golf Resort
Bandon, Oregon

Bandon Dunes Golf Resort
57744 Round Lake Drive
Bandon, OR 97411
Tel.: (888) 345-6008
Fax: (541) 347-5796
www.bandondunesgolf.com

Designer: **David McLay Kidd (Bandon Dunes); Tom Doak (Pacific Dunes)**

Date opened: **1999 (Bandon Dunes); 2001 (Pacific Dunes)**

Number of holes: **36, an 18-hole Ben Crenshaw course is in the works**

Fees: **$200**

Yardage/par: **6,732 yards, par-72 (Bandon Dunes); 7,557 yards, par-71 (Pacific Dunes)**

Rating/slope: **74.6/145 (Bandon Dunes); 72.9/133 (Pacific Dunes)**

Pro shop: **Bright and airy shop with plenty of logoed merchandise and equipment, and an emphasis on foul-weather gear**

Golf instruction: **For individual or group sessions**

Driving range/putting green: **The thirty-two-acre range allows players to work on all the knock-down shots they'll need to combat the wind; one-acre putting green gets you acclimated to some of the long putts you'll likely face**

Rentals: **Clubs**

A trip to Bandon Dunes Golf Resort is a special treat for the true golfer. It's not the kind of resort you visit for the peppermint scrub, chamomile cucumber eye peel, or licorice essence pedicure. This is where you go to play golf in North America's purest Scottish-style environment, where twenty-three miles of sweeping pristine shoreline await you. It's where you could be beaten up by wind and rain, stroll through sun-dappled days with the tall grasses waving as you walk by, or stare out at the Pacific Ocean as the whales frolic. Sometimes that all happens in the same round.

This is the place where you prove how much you want to visit. You've got to take the "planes, trains, and automobiles" route, but it is more than worth it to reach what has quickly become hallowed golf soil in the United States. Bandon Dunes is the kind of resort that inspires golfers to get all misty-eyed and wax poetic about the game's restorative powers.

Of course, Bandon Dunes draws inevitable comparisons to Pebble Beach, and the courses are similar. But the road splits when you get off the course. Pebble is Pebble, and the fabulous factor works there. But Bandon's charm is in its small scope. It is a welcome relief when all you want to do is play golf, chat about the round, play some more golf, eat, debate whether to get a massage or play another nine holes, fall asleep, and then get up and do it all again.

THE LODGING AT BANDON DUNES provides simple comfort to go with the pure golf experience. If you've never played courses in Scotland or Ireland, you are going to be catatonic after your rounds, so sleep is your friend. The Chrome Lake Rooms feature single king, double king, and two-room suites. The Lily Pond Rooms have two queen beds, while the Lodge offers single rooms and four suites, many with dramatic views of the golf course. There are two restaurants, two lounges, golf shops, a hot tub, sauna, and exercise room, and locker rooms. If you need a rubdown, you can get it, but because this isn't a spa-factory, you do need to plan in advance. Bandon Dunes is five minutes from the charming seaside town of Bandon, and about a half-hour from the North Bend Airport, which handles four flights from Portland. If you fly into North Bend, you can rent a car or be picked up by the resort's limo. I recommend the former; the latter will have more room than a rental, but it's just too pretentious to pull up to a resort such as this in a limo.

The Bandon Dunes (opposite page) and Pacific Dunes (this page) courses provide the purest form of U.S. golf unearthed in decades.

AT THE BANDON DUNES GOLF RESORT, guests are encouraged to play thirty-six holes per day. There is no charge for more than thirty-six holes per day. Does this tell you everything you need to know about this place? If it doesn't, here's another clue: They actually want you to walk and take a caddie, but you could also carry your own bag or take a trolley (again, a little bit of Scotland). As a matter of fact, you could wind up with the same caddie for the duration of your stay, which will help you score better because the caddie will have a feel for your game.

Bandon Dunes was set atop a series of sand dunes perched one hundred feet above the Pacific. Scotsman David McLay Kidd ran seven holes along the edge of the bluff overlooking the beach; you can see the ocean from every hole and get into a rhythm as you fall into step with the waves. The large fairways play firm and fast, and the sandy soil allows them to drain quickly even after a heavy rain. The holes are framed by tall grasses. The large greens allow creative players to keep the ball under the wind and roll the ball toward the hole.

Pacific Dunes might be the younger sibling here, but it has earned plenty of accolades in its brief life.

The Tom Doak design is shorter than Bandon, and is built on a site about half the distance from the beach as the older course. Somehow, though, emerging from shore pines to spectacular sixty-foot dunes blanketed in grasses and native vegetation feels even more natural. While the winds can still wreak havoc, it feels like you get more of a break down here. The green complexes are smaller, with more dramatic undulations, so while you still need to play those run-up shots into the green, the curves of the putting surfaces could push them in directions you hadn't planned for.

Left and above: The lodging at Bandon Dunes provides a simple place for golfers to rest their weary heads after a thirty-six-hole day of walking among the dunes and staying steady in the elements.

Sunriver Resort
Sunriver, Oregon

Sunriver Resort
One Center Drive
Sunriver, OR 97707
Tel.: (800) 801-8765
Fax: (541) 593-5458
www.sunriver-resort.com

Designer: **John Fought (Meadows Course); Robert Trent Jones Jr. (Woodlands Course); Robert Cupp (Crosswater Course)**

Date opened: **1969, with 1999 redesign (Meadows); 1982 (Woodlands); 1995 (Crosswater)**

Number of holes: **54**

Fees: **$60–$155**

Yardage/par: **7,012 yards/par-71 (Meadows); 6,880 yards/par-72 (Woodlands); 7,683 yards/par-72 (Crosswater)**

Rating/slope: **72.8/128 (Meadows); 73.0/131 (Woodlands); 76.7/150 (Crosswater)**

Pro shop: **Full pro shop at each course, offering equipment and apparel; through unique deal, only Nike products available at Woodlands shop**

Golf instruction: **For individual or group sessions at Ron Seals Academy of Golf; specific areas set up for putting, short-game, and full swing instruction**

Driving range/putting green: **Expansive area**

Rentals: **Clubs**

Clean air, check. Spectacular views of the Cascade Mountains, check. Three spectacular golf courses, check. Lodging that makes you feel like Grizzly Adams, and you don't even have to wrestle a bear or split a log, count me in. Did we mention that it is on the dry side of the Cascades? Sunriver Resort offers snowcapped mountains, pristine rivers, a nearly yearlong Northwest temperate climate, and an all-access pass to a 35,000-square-foot health club/spa. The resort features 209 rooms and suites, as well as thirty-three lodges, and also has a complex of 280 private homes and condos—many of the visitors become homeowners before they make their second trip back to this spectacular central Oregon staple.

Then there's the golf course, set at the base of the mountains on flat to gently rolling terrain that lets the ball fly through the crystalline air. The resort has captured the highest honors conveyed by publications as diverse as *Golf Magazine* and *Golf Digest* to *Family Fun* and *Wine Spectator*, proving that they have something for everyone.

ALTHOUGH THE COLDEST average high temperature dips just below forty degrees in January and December, the crisp air in this remarkable central Oregon destination makes guests want to schedule a full day of activities. From hiking to fishing to playing golf, or spending the day at the Sage Springs Club and Spa, you never run out of options here. As if the fresh air and outdoor action wasn't enough to lower your blood pressure, the spa's services—the Hazelnut Scrub/Deep-Tissue Massage, High Desert Wrapsody/Oasis Massage, or Sage Springs Essential Riverside Relaxer Massage—should give you an all-is-right-with-the-world glow.

Returning from a day's worth of outdoor activities to a room with a fireplace is not an overrated option, but don't get too comfortable in front of the fire or you'll miss the many events happening downstairs. The resort's hub, the Lodge, is the place to go for a meal, shopping, or just hanging out. The casual atmosphere lets you dress down-home but eat in uptown style. Meadows at the Lodge provides fine dining and an award-winning wine list, while the Owl's Nest is the perfect spot for a Northwest microbrew, a light meal, and some live music.

Left: Robert Trent Jones Jr.'s use of water and natural terrain make the Woodlands Course one of the most difficult at Sunriver Resort. Above: The Lodge is the hub for dining and social activities once the sun goes down.

SUNRIVER RESORT's remarkable surroundings can't guarantee that you'll play your best golf. But if you do manage to miss a shot (or six), take a look at the snowcap on nearby Mount Bachelor and you'll no doubt realize that losing your mind over golf can wait until you get back home to your pals. The courses at Sunriver provide different sets of challenges. Crosswater, designed by Bob Cupp, is a brawny sprawling 7,683 yards and spooky 76.7 rating. While the flat terrain and wide fairways make you comfortable from the teebox, there isn't a par-3 shorter than 180 yards and when the par-4s continue to stretch beyond 480 yards, the 635-yard sixth and 687-yard twelfth holes almost seem manageable. In addition to the respect the course has earned from the biggest hitters, Crosswater also has earned a designation as a certified Audubon Sanctuary, one of only 150 U.S. courses to have been so honored. This is where you can supply your own joke about seeing birdies if you can't make one.

The Meadows was the first course built at Sunriver, in 1969. John Fought, architect and former U.S. Amateur Champion, has just completed a total redesign, and the course now runs along the Sun River and through stands of pines. Fought tried to take the course even farther back in time, approximating the simple lines of designs from the 1920s and 1930s. Make it through the watery second, third, and fourth holes with enough pellets to finish the round and you should be home free—until you get to the 467-yard dogleg-left eighteenth.

Robert Trent Jones Jr.'s Woodlands Course at Sunriver spends some quality time winding through pine-lined fairways. It opens up on the back nine, where his strategic use of water and large bunkers places a premium on accuracy.

If you make it through your round here on the slick greens without any major catastrophes, you might want to have a little fun and tackle the nine-hole bent-grass putting course. At 691 feet, you won't have to worry about either carrying your golf bag or losing any more balls.

Above: The Meadows Course was the first course built for Sunriver.
Right: With snowcapped Mt. Bachelor in the background, the nine-hole putting course is the perfect place to settle any post-round disputes.

The Fairmont Chateau Whistler
Whistler, British Columbia, Canada

The Fairmont Chateau Whistler
4599 Chateau Boulevard
Whistler, BC, Canada VoN 1B4
Tel.: (604) 938-8000
Fax: (604) 938-2291
www.fairmont.com

Designer: **Robert Trent Jones Jr.**

Date opened: **1993**

Number of holes: **18**

Fees: **$45–$95, $15 for juniors eighteen years of age or younger**

Yardage/par: **6,635 yards, par-72**

Rating/slope: **73.1/131**

Pro shop: **You'll notice the "merchandiser of the year" awards hanging on the walls of the shop, which means that you should be able to find anything you need, from balls and clubs to apparel**

Golf instruction: **For individual or group sessions, Canada's only David Leadbetter Golf Academy provides one- to four-day schools that can be tailored to golfers' needs**

Driving range/putting green: **Double-tiered, 350-yard range; 10,000-square-foot short game area with putting green, practice bunkers, and chipping areas**

Rentals: **Clubs and shoes**

After a two-hour drive from Vancouver along the spectacular Sea to Sky Highway, you'll get to The Fairmont Chateau Whistler and feel a sense of wonderment at this resort in the Upper Whistler village. The sprawling complex, set right at the foot of Whistler Mountain (where you will see the world's best skiers participate in the 2010 Olympics), is managed by the same company that pampers guests at the Plaza Hotel in New York City. There is an air of confidence and competence among the staff members here and a sense of European repose, whether at the scenic and challenging golf course designed by Robert Trent Jones Jr., in the resort itself, or in the casual way in which guests saunter to and from Whistler proper for food, shopping, cocktails, or any combination of the three.

Condé Nast Traveler has named Whistler the top ski resort in North America based on its one hundred marked runs and vertical height of more than seven thousand feet. It probably didn't hurt that there is helicopter service for skiers wishing to be dropped in specific areas. When the praise rolled in for the golf course, which was opened in 1993, it made the resort a full-fledged year-round destination, the kind of place that the worldly golfer will be visiting in a variety of seasons.

THE FAIRMONT CHATEAU WHISTLER is the kind of vacation destination where the truly ambitious can bring travel bags full of both golf clubs and ski equipment. Guests may even lug their mountain bikes just in case there is some sort of natural convergence that will allow them to show just how versatile and fit they are.

Offering fine variations on the Pacific Northwest dining theme, The Wildflower and Portobello are two restaurants offering high-end options. The Wildflower offers guests a wine list that boasts more than 250 Canadian and international wines. True wine lovers can also request to have a dinner seating in the Wildflower Wine Room, which can accommodate eighteen people in a floor-to-ceiling windowed room that provides views out of Whistler Mountain.

The commitment to mind and body goes beyond the outdoor activities. The fitness center has everything you need to get stronger and run farther. The Willow Stream Spa has a heated lap pool with music piped in underwater; there are eucalyptus steam rooms, and a mandate to help visitors restore a sense of inner calm, outer vitality, sensory pleasure, and spiritual health. The Swedana Steam Treatment starts with a massage and concludes with a session in a cedar steam cabinet, giving your body a steam while your head is exposed to cooler air. After you get out of the cabinet, you will be given a dusting of flour to help prevent toxins from reentering your body. Even children get pampered here with a massage that the Whistler folks insist, "strengthens the immune system, tones skin, aids digestion, and relieves growing pains." (They even chart muscular and postural analysis and provide take-home instructions for stretching and strengthening muscles.) Could it also get them to take out the trash?

At nearly nine thousand feet above sea level, the wonders of the Whistler experience include blooming purple lupines and snowcapped mountains (far left), great hiking at nearby Cheakamus Lake (left, top), or the verdant par-4 third hole (left, bottom).

THE COURSE AT THE FAIRMONT CHATEAU WHISTLER boasts dramatic elevation changes of four hundred feet. Anywhere else, that sort of rise and fall would be spectacular, but when the course is built in the shadow of Blackcomb and Whistler mountains, it seems kind of like a quick jaunt down the bunny slope. That said, this is some of the most rugged and beautiful countryside any course has been cut from. The course opened four years after the resort welcomed its first guest and has quickly caught on with golfers, especially the outdoorsy types who don't mind going out for a brisk post-golf walk in the woods.

The course isn't overly challenging, but keeping your focus on the task at hand should be added into the slope and course rating. The 457-yard dogleg-left sixth hole is a bear, featuring a green that has a couple of ridges that push the ball in surprising directions. The dogleg-right 472-yard par-5 ninth is a great birdie opportunity that could catapult you into a low number on the back nine, but if you mess with the left side of the fairway and its eight bunkers you've got no chance to get home in two. The closing hole is a testy 543-yard par-5 that is fairly open for the first two shots but tightens significantly into a green that is guarded to the right by towering pines and to the left by bunkers. It's a good news/bad news dilemma: the thin air will give you more carry on the ball, but you might be so winded in the altitude that you can't muster the energy to give it a big poke and get home in two.

The close proximity of snow-capped hiking trails in Garibaldi Provincial Park (above) and the majestic backdrop of Whistler Mountain at the par-5 seventh hole (right) provide an incredible fresh perspective.

Index

The American Club, **122**
444 Highland Drive
Kohler, WI 53044
Tel.: (800) 344-2838
Fax: (920) 457-0299
www.destinationkohler.com

Bandon Dunes Golf Resort, **188**
57744 Round Lake Drive
Bandon, OR 97411
Tel.: (888) 345-6008
Fax: (541) 347-5796
www.bandondunesgolf.com

The Boulders, **76**
34631 North Tom Darlington Drive
P.O. Box 2090
Carefree, AZ 85377
Tel.: (800) 553-1717
or (480) 488-9009
Fax: (702) 567-4777
www.wyndham.com

The Broadmoor, **70**
One Lake Avenue
Colorado Springs, CO 80906
Tel.: (800) 634-7711
or (719) 577-5775
Fax: (719) 577-5738
www.broadmoor.com

Coeur d'Alene Resort, **182**
115 South 2nd Street
Coeur d'Alene, ID 83814
Tel.: (800) 688-5253
Fax: (208) 664-7276
www.cdaresort.com

The Equinox, **10**
3567 Main Street
Manchester Village, VT 05254
Tel.: (800) 362-4747
Fax: (802) 362-4700
www.equinoxresort.com

The Fairmont Chateau Whistler, **200**
4599 Chateau Boulevard
Whistler, BC, Canada VoN 1B4
Tel.: (604) 938-8000
Fax: (604) 938-2291
www.fairmont.com

Four Seasons Resort Aviara, **134**
7100 Four Seasons Point
Carlsbad, CA 92009
Tel.: (760) 603-6800
Fax: (760) 603-6801
www.fourseasons.com/aviara

Four Seasons Resort Scottsdale
at Troon North, **82**
10600 East Crescent Moon Drive
Scottsdale, AZ 85262
Tel.: (480) 515-5700
Fax: (480) 515-5599
www.fourseasons.com/scottsdale

Golden Horseshoe Golf Club, **30**
401 South England Street
Williamsburg, VA 23188
Tel.: (757) 220-7696
Fax: (757) 565-8840
www.colonialwilliamsburg.com

Grand Cypress Resort, **62**
One North Jacaranda
Orlando, FL 32836
Tel.: (407) 239-4700
Fax: (407) 239-1969
www.grandcypress.com

Grand View Lodge, **176**
23521 Nokomis
Nisswa, MN 56468
Tel.: (800) 432-3788
Fax: (218) 963-2269
www.grandviewlodge.com

Grand Wailea Resort
Hotel & Spa, **94**
3850 Wailea Alanui
Wailea, Maui, HI 96753
Tel.: (808) 875-1234
Fax: (808) 879-4077
www.grandwailea.com

The Greenbrier, **42**
300 West Main Street
White Sulphur Springs, WV 24986
Tel.: (800) 453-4858
Fax: (304) 536-7854
www.greenbrier.com

The Hershey Resort, **24**
100 Hotel Road
Hershey, PA 17033
Tel.: (800) HERSHEY
Fax: (717) 534-8887
www.hersheypa.com

The Homestead, **36**
U.S. Route 220
Main Street
Hot Springs, VA 24445
Tel.: (800) 838-1766
or (540) 839-1766
Fax: (540) 839-1670
www.thehomestead.com

Hyatt Regency Kauai
Resort and Spa, **98**
1571 Poipu Road
Koloa, HI 96756
Tel.: (808) 742-1234
Fax: (808) 742-1557
www.kauai.hyatt.com

The Inn at Spanish Bay, **140**
2700 17-Mile Drive
Pebble Beach, CA 93953
Tel.: (800) 654-9300
Fax: (831) 622-3603
www.pebblebeach.com

Kiawah Island Golf Resort, **110**
12 Kiawah Beach Drive
Kiawah Island, SC 29455
Tel.: (800) 576-1570
Fax: (843) 768-6093
www.kiawahresort.com

La Quinta Resort & Club, **88**
49–499 Eisenhower Drive
La Quinta, CA 92253
Tel.: (800) 598-3828
Fax: (760) 564-5768
www.laquintaresort.com

Nemacolin Woodlands
Resort & Spa, **104**
1001 LaFayette Drive
Farmington, PA 15437
Tel.: (800) 422-2736
Fax: (724) 329-8555
www.nemacolin.com

One&Only Palmilla, **158**
Km 7.5 Carretera
Transpeninsular
San Jose Del Cabo
BCS, CP 23400 Mexico
Tel.: (800) 637-2226
Fax: 011-52-624-146-7001
www.oneandonlyresorts.com

Pebble Beach Golf Links, **144**
1700 17-Mile Drive
Pebble Beach, CA 93953
Tel.: (800) 654-9300
Fax: (831) 625-8598
www.pebblebeach.com

Pinehurst Resort, **46**
80 Carolina Vista
Village of Pinehurst, NC 28374
Tel.: (800) ITSGOLF
Fax: (910) 235-8466
www.pinehurst.com

Ponte Vedra Inn & Club, **66**
200 Ponte Vedra Boulevard
Ponte Vedra Beach, FL 32082
Tel.: (800) 234-7842
Fax: (904) 285-2111
www.pvresorts.com

Princeville Resort, **154**
5520 Ka Haku Road
P.O. Box 223069
Princeville, Kauai, HI 96722
Tel.: (800) 826-9644
Fax: (808) 826-1166
www.princeville.com

Photo Credits

The Ritz-Carlton Lodge,
Reynolds Plantation, **116**
One Lake Oconee Trail
Greensboro, GA 30642
Tel.: (706) 467-0600
Fax: (706) 467-0601
www.ritz-carlton.com

The Ritz-Carlton Golf & Spa
Resort, Rose Hall, **164**
One Ritz-Carlton Drive
Rose Hall
St. James, Jamaica
West Indies
Tel.: (876) 953-2800
Fax: (876) 953-2501
www.ritz-carlton.com

The Ritz-Carlton,
Half Moon Bay, **148**
One Miramontes Point Road
Half Moon Bay, CA 94019
Tel.: (650) 712-7000
Fax: (650) 712-7070
www.ritz-carlton.com

The Ritz-Carlton,
Lake Las Vegas, **128**
1610 Lake Las Vegas Parkway
Henderson, NV 89011
Tel.: (800) 241-3333
or (702) 567-4700
Fax: (702) 567-4777
www.ritz-carlton.com

The Sagamore, **14**
110 Sagamore Road
Bolton Landing, NY 12814
Tel.: (800) 358-3585
Fax: (518) 743-6036
www.thesagamore.com

Sea Island Resort, **58**
Tel.: (800) SEAISLAND
Fax: (912) 638-5159
www.seaisland.com

Seaview Marriott
Resort & Spa, **18**
401 South New York Road
Galloway Township, NJ 08205
Tel.: (609) 652-1800
Fax: (609) 652-2307
www.seaviewgolf.com

Sunriver Resort, **194**
One Center Drive
Sunriver, OR 97707
Tel.: (800) 801-8765
Fax: (541) 593-5458
www.sunriver-resort.com

Westin Rio Mar Beach
Resort & Golf Club, **168**
6000 Rio Mar Boulevard
Rio Grande, PR 00745-6100
Tel.: (888) 627-8556
Fax: (787) 888-6600
www.westinriomar.com

Wild Dunes Resort, **52**
5757 Palm Boulevard
Isle of Palms, SC 29451
Tel.: (888) 845-8926
Fax: (843) 886-2916
www.wilddunes.com

Acknowledgments

I must extend heartfelt thanks to Dan Husted, who supplied original photography and a consuming commitment to detail that he doesn't see as abnormal (that's OK, we can get him in a program). Tom Mackin, entrusted with the thankless task of shepherding countless photos to their final docking station, provided the calm in a crazy time. My editor, Jane Ginsberg, was an invaluable source of expertise and an unwavering supporter of this project. Adam Michaels spent countless hours designing, tweaking, and tinkering with the layout of the book until it satisfied his discerning eye. Tiffany Sprague pored over the manuscript, copyediting it to perfection. And to just some of my friends in golf—Jim and John Andrews, Brett Avery, Joe Bargmann, Ken Cohen, Michael Corcoran, Tom Dellner, Steve Donahue, Jim Frank, Terry Golway, Jim Gorant, Sam Greenwood, Dove Jones, Scott Kramer, Eamon Lynch, Chris Millard, Karen Moraghan, Cameron Morfit, Kevin Morris, Jack O'Leary, Joe Passov, George Peper, Mike Purkey, Tom and Tod Rittenhouse, Evan Rothman, Tony Roberts, and Ken van Kampen—your stories and our shared experiences are worth a set of books.

Compiling the information in the following pages would have been impossible without the help of the many marketing and public relations professionals from each of these resorts. Completion of the book would have also occurred at a snail's pace without referencing *Golf Resorts of the World: The Best Places to Stay and Play*, by Brian McCallen.

There aren't enough ways to thank Paula, who inspires me each day with a brilliance, love, creativity, and patience that I don't deserve. And to our boys, Zachary and Luke; if they pursue this game with even a fraction of the love and joy they give us, they will share a bond of brotherhood and never-ending memories. Of course, none of this would ever have been possible without the love and support of my parents, George and Rhoann, who together instilled a commitment to love and loyalty, as well as a never-ending desire for just nine more holes, in Mark, Dick, Megan, and me.